How Not to Fall Apart

HOW NOT TO FALL APART

Lessons Learned on the Road from Self-Harm to Self-Care

MAGGY VAN EIJK

A TarcherPerigee Book

tarcherperigee

An imprint of Penguin Random House LLC
375 Hudson Street
New York, New York 10014

Most TarcherPerigee books are available at special quantity discounts for bulk purchase for sales promotions, premiums, fund-raising, and educational needs. Special books or book excerpts also can be created to fit specific needs. For details, write: SpecialMarkets@penguinrandomhouse.com.

Library of Congress Cataloging-in-Publication Data

Names: Van Eijk, Maggy, author.
Title: How not to fall apart : lessons learned on the road from self-harm to self-care / Maggy van Eijk.
Description: New York, New York : TarcherPerigee, [2018] |
Identifiers: LCCN 2018022861 (print) | LCCN 2018029537 (ebook) |
ISBN 9780525505280 | ISBN 9780143133490 (paperback)
Subjects: LCSH: Mentally health. | Mental health—Treatment. |
Self-care, Health. | BISAC: SELF-HELP / Depression. |
PSYCHOLOGY / Mental Health.
Classification: LCC RA790 (ebook) | LCC RA790 .V33 2018 (print) |
DDC 616.89—dc23
LC record available at https://lccn.loc.gov/2018022861
p.   cm.

Printed in the United States of America
1   3   5   7   9   10   8   6   4   2

For Annie and Sandy

This book made me feel less alone in a single page.
It's reassuring, warm, hilarious, and without a doubt will help
countless other people feel less alone as well, which is
the best thing any book about mental health can do.

MEGAN CRABBE @BODY

CONTENTS

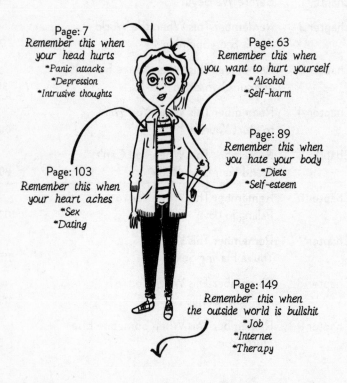

Page: 7
Remember this when your head hurts
*Panic attacks
*Depression
Intrusive thoughts

Page: 63
Remember this when you want to hurt yourself
*Alcohol
Self-harm

Page: 103
Remember this when your heart aches
*Sex
Dating

Page: 89
Remember this when you hate your body
*Diets
Self-esteem

Page: 149
Remember this when the outside world is bullshit
*Job
*Internet
Therapy

How Not to Fall Apart

CHAPTER 1

Before We Begin

s this a good idea?"

"Is this a good idea?"

"Are we sure this is a good idea?"

This is the conversation I have with myself the most, sometimes out loud in the futile hope someone out there will reply. I said it when I told my doctor about my anxiety, I said it when I swallowed my first dose of Citalopram, I said it when I took myself to the ER, and I said it when I was thinking about writing this book.

Is it a good idea to write about something I'm still very much in the middle of? It feels like writing about war when I'm still on the battlefield or reporting on an earthquake when shockwaves are tearing down houses around me.

Deep down I know that writing this book *is* a good idea because it's what's helping me continue on. I have a Quality Street tin of mental health conditions that sometimes decide to get together and make a joint appearance. One condition at a time is relatively manageable but when they all flare up at once it feels like I'm walking around with my head on fire. Only no one can see the blaze. Apart from the scars that run up and down my arms like a train track, everything looks calm. Business as usual.

I hope that by writing my story, by turning my brain inside out and making the invisible visible, I can help someone in a similar position, someone who feels they're stuck in the trenches and there's no way out. What I've learned so far is that no matter how shitty your situation is, there is an escape route, and every time you climb out you'll be more equipped to deal with the next falling down. This book aims to remind people of that, and myself too.

No matter how shitty your situation is, there is an escape route.

Ultimately, your mental illness lies to you. It'll tell you that everything is wrong and that you have no future. It'll tell

2

you that you should be ashamed and you're a nuisance and you don't deserve to get help. The world in which depression and anxiety reign supreme is extremely lonely, and I wanted to write this book to reach out and say: "Hey there, you're not alone, I'm right there with you."

Having said that, everyone's mind is unique, and while our background and diagnoses might sound similar, my story can't encompass your entire experience. In fact, diagnoses can be a strange thing. I was told I had unipolar depression at age seventeen, then a doctor came along and added bipolar to the mix in my early twenties, another one went back to the original conclusion, and finally, aged twenty-seven I was told I have borderline personality disorder. Each time I received a new diagnosis, I assumed I'd step out of my doctor's office and my entire life would change, but it never did. Instead, my mental health remained the same tough slog of a thing I have to push through to move forward.

This book isn't specifically about my borderline personality disorder, but it might touch on symptoms of that condition. I'll also touch on depression, anxiety, self-harm, and self-esteem while moving through my body—the head, the skin, the heart—and the world around me. I'll talk about the moments we all have when you're stressed, angry, sad, or all three. When you're plummeting into a sinkhole. When you feel so lost you could do with a map that tells you where you are and where you're most likely going to be tomorrow.

Depression is in no way equal to "sadness," but I am sad an awful lot. So I've also filled this book with little everyday reminders to pull myself out of my brain ditch. There are notes and anecdotes plastered all over my walls, my phone, my notebook, my mirror, and the back of my hand, and I've put them all together on paper in a way I hope you'll find useful. Some of these reminders are set up as lists. I love lists. They impose a sense of organization onto a lot of the chaos that whizzes around in my head. I make daily to-do lists. I make them for work. I make them for when I get home. I make bigger picture lists: week goals, month goals, year goals. I also have lists for things to reward myself with: tattoos, books, films, playlists.

The most important aspect of lists for me is the fact that they are a direct link to the future, even if it's as immediate as what I'm going to be doing in the next half hour. Lists tell me I need to hang on. They tell me not to give up just yet, which is why I'm using them so often in this book. Hopefully they'll have the same effect on you too.

While I hope to offer you the best advice I can, it's important to remember that there is no blueprint for experiencing a mental health problem. There's no one-size-fits-all solution either. Personally, I've found reading about others' experiences to be enlightening and comforting, so I hope this book can achieve that for you. If anything you read makes you feel stressed out or uncomfortable, make sure you speak out and ask for help.

Now let's begin.

CHAPTER 2

Remember This When the World Won't Stop Spinning

PANIC AT THE DISCO

I'm twenty years old standing at the top of Row Mead and I'm about to die. Amy Winehouse has appeared on Glastonbury's Pyramid Stage. She weaves a halo over Worthy Farm with her booming voice and erratic yet hypnotizing movements. She's singing "Back to Black" and I'm trying to drink in the words that I've come to know so well, but there's a problem—something awful is happening to me. I'm pretty sure I'm dying.

Between "Cupid" and "Back to Black," my legs had turned to jelly, my stomach somersaulted, acidic dread had climbed up my throat, and as I fell toward the muddy grass I hoped someone would tell my family I loved them, because this was it. At the very least I was losing my mind; at the worst my life was about to end.

I opened my eyes and realized I was somehow not quite dead yet. My boyfriend, P., lifted me up and carried me to the medical tent, assuring me along the way that yes I was still breathing. The nurse handed me a plastic cup of water and suggested I go lie down in my tent and lay off the Ecstasy. I wanted to tell her I'd never done drugs in my whole life, but something told me she wouldn't believe me. I was ushered back outside, where Amy was still playing somewhere in the distance.

I hoped my weird dizzy spell was a fluke, but we had to cut our Glastonbury trip short: whether I was standing in a crowd of Kings of Leon fans or waiting for falafel in front of a food truck, I kept experiencing that surge of feeling, like my-life-is-ending-right-this-second. I was constantly sprinting back to our tent to cry and hyperventilate into my sleeping bag.

When I left Glastonbury and returned to my student life in Bristol, I convinced myself that whatever happened at the festival was the result of dehydration or perhaps a dodgy sandwich. But then a couple of days later it hit me again on the bus, then again in the student union bar, and again in lectures and one-on-one tutorials. In the moments between attacks I didn't feel right either. I felt disconnected from everything around me like my head was stuck in a snow globe. I barged into the doctor's convinced I had diabetes, a brain tumor, chronic fatigue, an iron deficiency, vertigo, meningitis, Ebola, Alice in Wonderland syndrome (yes, this is a thing), migraines, IBS, and meningitis again. I did test after test, but I was constantly told that I was in perfect health. During my fifty-sixth trip to the doctor, a new GP saw me. He asked how often I drank alcohol: "barely ever." And how often did I do drugs: "never." He put his pen down on his desk.

"I know I'm not supposed to say this, but you're a student, and that's sort of what students do."

"I don't like going out."

"Why?"

"I don't know. I don't like it."

"Do you have many friends?"

"Um, no."

He swiveled his chair around to face me. I felt that familiar dizziness again. My mind began to drift out of my body and the painted sailboat on the wall seemed to rock back and forth.

"Have you ever been diagnosed with depression or anxiety?"

"I saw a psychologist when I was a teenager, but that was because I used to self-harm."

"And now?"

"Not really."

"Not really?"

9

"I don't self-harm as much."

He gave me a stack of leaflets, some URLs that were scribbled on Post-its, and told me to have a read and get back to him. On my walk home I toyed with this new idea. Maybe I didn't have a terminal illness; maybe whatever I had was—mental?

While I had seen a psychologist as a teenager, those sessions were back in the Netherlands, where I'm from. The term "anxiety" had never been mentioned, even though I do remember discussing the feeling. The word in its English form seemed floaty. I kind of knew what it was, but not really. What actually *is* anxiety? What does it look like? How can you stop something you don't understand?

For me, anxiety is like having a crystal ball, but the ball is distorted and cloudy and everything in there is the most messed-up version of events. For example, "I can see that my future holds a work presentation and I bet I'll shit my pants and vomit on my boss and I'll never work in media ever again!"

The following week my doctor gave me the official diagnosis of generalized anxiety disorder. While coming to terms with anxiety as something I was dealing with, I realized how cruel a condition it is. Yes, it's in your mind, but it feels extremely physical. My symptoms include sweating, trembling, heart palpitations, and nausea. The nausea has always been my least favorite of the bunch; it's that horrible dragging feeling in the pit of my stomach that will stay long after the

stressful event is over. It makes me feel like I'm constantly on the verge of puking, but nothing will ever come out of my throat. At university, the nausea developed into emetophobia (a fear of vomiting) and prevented me from showing up to classes, going to pubs, and even just leaving the house. I was in permanent fear that I'd puke wherever I went. Sometimes I'd get on the bus, only to have to get off again after one stop and walk home. I couldn't handle the rest of the twenty-minute journey.

I've also fainted and almost fainted a dozen times because of anxiety. I end up sending myself into such a whirlpool of worry and panic that my breathing spirals out of control, I feel dizzy, I start hyperventilating, and *boom*, I'm on the floor.

While I was never in any actual immediate danger (apart from the time I fainted at the hairdresser and she almost stabbed me in the head with her scissors), I genuinely believe that in that moment I am going to die. It's the thing people really underestimate about panic attacks. It's not a matter of "just calm down." You can't, because it feels like you're trapped inside your own body, and the only escape is the relief you'll feel when the light finally goes out. You *will* die. There's no other option. It's terrifying.

But then when you do come out the other side, you live in constant fear that it's going to *happen again*. Any hint of nausea, mild dizziness, or a shaky hand and it's all systems go in my head. I imagine a bunch of army men running around preparing for battle: "She's about to blow, fellas! All hands on deck!" There's also that lingering feeling of shame after I survive an attack. When you were so certain you were about to die and yet you're still very much alive, it can feel like a slight anticlimax. Not that I wanted to die, but I'm embarrassed I genuinely thought I would and yet here I am—blood pumping, heart racing.

I've had anxiety in places that were so mundane and boring I'd never expected my body to unleash such an extreme reaction. In an Asda in Bristol during the height of my anxiety, I attempted to go food shopping with my boyfriend, P. It was one of those enormous Asdas where it seems like there's an endless stream of garish lights dotting aisle after aisle after aisle. I'm always afraid that in large supermarkets or shopping malls I'll get swallowed up; I'll be stuck in an aisle and never get out. Supermarkets feel like a mangled maze, and there's no place to stop for a rest. You have to keep going, right to the till, where if you're not fast enough you'll hold up all the people behind you.

P. walked ahead of me, ticking off the list of groceries I had meticulously made. Thanks to my fear of puking everywhere, I didn't really socialize at university, so I had a lot of time to do things like make a joint food plan to last us a week. I'd organize the list in food groups, making it easier to find in the supermarket. I'd then calculate exactly how much the items would cost and split them down the middle so we'd each pay half. P. didn't really mind my food shopping dictatorship. It meant he saved money and didn't have to worry about what he was eating for dinner.

So we were in Asda and had only just made it to the fresh food section when I felt the panic settle in. I stopped in my tracks. The bright supermarket lights seemed to merge to form a wild tidal wave about to crash on top of me. I passed the shopping list to P. like we were soldiers in an epic war movie and I was handing over a picture of my wife and kids to my comrade before taking my last breath: "Go forth, be brave and please tell my wife I love her."

To the outside, I probably looked relatively normal. As P. went off into battle, I decided to find an aisle that was less busy. I found the entertainment section and picked up one of Britney Spears' unofficial biographies while my vision blurred and turned to blue. I slumped to the ground but managed to hoist myself into a sitting position. I felt like everyone was staring at me, so I grabbed the book and pretended to read. I sat there until P. collected me and we walked home. I felt defeated and silly and stupid and refused to talk about what happened. I spent the rest of the evening in bed.

I've had other panic attacks in situations that were more unfortunate than Asda. My personal favorite being the one I had a year and a half after Asda-gate. P. and I had broken up. We'd been dating for eight years, and had grown up together and barely left each other's sides. I was alone now and I had no idea how all this worked, this dating stuff. How would I meet someone new?

I had the very unglamorous job of being an usher in a theater in the West End. The Casanova of my colleagues, a guy I'll call R.—dark hair, suave—began to flirt with me. I could just about manage the flirting and reciprocated whenever I felt brave enough. When he eventually asked after a night in the pub if I wanted to go back to his flat, I thought I'd received the golden ticket. This is what single life is like, I cheered. Handsome guys ask you to go back to their house and you do that because you can—this is great!

Well, not really. Nerves cluttered my brain and I started to do that annoying thing I often do in the presence of men I want to impress where I hide away my personality and become a cardboard version of myself, hoping that I project whatever it is they want from me. "Please like me please like me please like me," pleaded my brain as we took the Tube back to his place. A fight broke out in our car between a toothless man and a businessman in a gray suit. Allegedly, toothless man had had an accident and may or may not have shat himself. Businessman was screaming in his face telling him he was disgusting and should get off the train and go shower.

I really should have taken this as an omen for the night to come (don't worry, I didn't quite shit myself).

R. and I got into his flat and watched some *Alan Partridge*, which guys often like doing when they find out I'm foreign (it's that, followed by *The Office*, followed by *Fawlty Towers*, followed by *Blackadder*). After this we retreated to his bedroom, where I focused on being a totally cool, sexy girl and not at all awkward or weird. This was my first time sleeping with someone new after eight years of being with the same person. What if my body was ugly? What if my vagina was weird? What if I smelled bad?

We got to it, which I know is a very unsexy way of describing sex, but I genuinely can't remember if it was any good because I was so goddamn stressed. When it was over he muttered something about not normally sleeping with people he's not properly dating, and I said, "Oh yeah, same," even though what I meant to say was: "Wait, what? What is happening? Is this a one-night thing? Do I go home? What do I do?" He shut his eyes and seemed to fall asleep immediately, so I shut my eyes too. I somehow managed to sleep, even though my body was so tense I was lying there like a corpse in a freezer.

I woke up in the middle of the night needing to pee. At the time he shared a flat with his sister and her now husband, which probably added to my nerves. The thought of bumping into them filled me with dread. Would I introduce myself? Would they think I was some floozy? Would they think I was an intruder? "Just get the peeing over with and run back to the room," I told myself. Seemed like a pretty simple plan, until I'd made myself so tense and stressed out I couldn't pee. Nothing was happening, despite the fact that my bladder was achingly full. Horror struck. "Fuck," I thought, "my bladder isn't working anymore."

I tried to think about running water, I turned the tap on and quietly started humming TLC's "Waterfalls," but no luck. Here I was, butt naked on the loo apart from an old wrestling T-shirt R. had lent me, freaking out that my body was going to fill up with urine and eventually explode.

I decided to give up on the whole urinating thing. I felt dizzy and panicky and I needed to go back to the bed and lie down. I flushed anyway so no one would get suspicious and left the bathroom. Somewhere halfway down this tiny corridor the bones in my legs turned to mulch. Despite the darkness, my vision became all dotted and turquoise. I just wanted to make it to the bedroom, but my body wasn't working with me. Before I knew it I was on the floor, and on my way down I'd managed to bash my cheek on his sister's bike. The

poor guy ran out of his room and saw me sprawled across the carpet, at which point I raised a very meek don't-worry-it's-all-OK thumbs-up.

He then sort of semidragged me back to his bedroom and put me to bed while I kept trying to tell him how sorry I was. With a throbbing cheek and a bladder full of pee, I tried to force sleep on myself. I couldn't. Luckily it was 4 a.m. I just needed to wait two more hours when it would be acceptable to leave. On leaving his house I gave him a high five and walked my way to Southfields train station. I got off halfway back to my house before finding a Starbucks to finally pee in. When I did it felt like I was peeing fire, but it still felt good. The tension in my body eased a little.

To my great surprise, we ended up seeing each other again. After this escapade, we even dated for a year and a bit. I learned that things I consider to be *end-of-the-world* dramatic affairs really aren't so dramatic for other people. Fainting in someone's corridor isn't really that much of a big deal, and in hindsight it's pretty funny.

Asda and postsex panic attacks are two pretty extreme reactions I've had thanks to anxiety caused by generally not feeling comfortable in certain situations. On a day-to-day basis, anxiety can shapeshift and manifest in lots of different ways. It's a constant presence; a cloud that won't leave you alone or a whisper in your ear that won't go away.

> Anxiety can shapeshift and manifest in lots of different ways.

Here's what a bad anxiety day looks like:

- Waking up in the middle of the night to remember that thing I said five years ago that probably came across as a bit rude. Time to linger on that memory until sunrise!
- Waking up to mentally list all the people I'm pretty sure hate me and why they hate me and what happened if I bumped into them in the street
- Leaving the house only to go back in again because it feels like a ton of bricks are falling down on my head
- Bopping my knee up and down so fast people walk by my desk to ask if I'm OK

- Having a bath to try to relax but then remembering the bath is basically an open coffin filled with my own liquid filth
- Hearing that voice in my head that follows me around and tells me what a pile of trash I am
- Laughing at something a coworker says only to then stop laughing because I sound like a goat and people must hate the sound of me
- Having a nice time with someone while also being convinced they secretly hate me
- Having to consult six friends about whether that one text I sent one of our other friends was perhaps a bit inappropriate and are we absolutely 100 percent positive they don't think I'm a freak?
- When it's a bit humid outside and it feels like oxygen is slowly being sucked out of the world and there isn't enough and dear god why is everyone else breathing freely like this?
- Having a knot of fear erupt at the base of my spine, then shooting up my body until I'm covered in a film of sweat and I have no idea why my body is reacting like this because I was just sitting here reading an email
- Seeing a pile of clothes in the dark and thinking it looks like a massive panther, then thinking, "Holy shit, what if it is a panther?" followed by, "Holy shit, the fact that you think it's a panther means you're probably losing your mind."

- Mentally saying good-bye to that guy you're really enjoying spending time with because you'll probably fuck it up anyway
- Receiving a very small amount of criticism at work, and instead of dealing with it by doing better at the next task, spending the whole day Googling new jobs because this is it, *they will fire you*

This is what a good anxiety day looks like:

- Getting up well rested because I was actually able to sleep
- Getting up and reading a book before I have to start the day because I've given myself enough time to slowly get out of bed and not bolt out the door
- Sitting in a meeting and not worrying about projectile vomiting on anyone
- Going for a swim not because I think my butt is too fat but because I genuinely fancy moving my body
- Losing track of time on the Tube because I'm listening to a true crime podcast and I'm completely absorbed and not imagining death by stampede in the car
- Having lunch in the office cafeteria and being able to enjoy my cheese sandwich because I don't feel like my head's about to disconnect from my body
- Tweeting something and not deleting it because I'm worried it's too lame/weird/annoying
- Going home and not drinking a bottle of wine by myself but instead making a meal that has actual vegetables in it

- Going home and not regretting fifteen hundred alleged mistakes I made that day
- Making a list of things I want to achieve over the rest of the year because I'm genuinely excited about the future
- Acknowledging that my body is not my enemy, it just overreacts to things sometimes, and that's OK
- Texting a friend to make a plan without the fear that they'll inevitably cancel because who would want to hang out with me anyway
- Tidying up my room because I want to live in a calm space, not on top of a mountain of clothes and dishes

I sort of have a handle on my day-to-day anxiety, but I am yet to go back to Glastonbury. I have made progress though; after years of avoiding concerts, cinemas, and plays, I can get through a festival pretty much OK now. A lot of preparation has to take place, and it's important I'm around people I feel like I can trust and be honest with. If things get wobbly I have to be able to leave without feeling like I'm letting anyone down. I have to have plenty of water on me, and ideally I prefer not to stand right in the middle of a crowd.

21

Here's some other ways I've learned how to survive a show:

- I always find the more you know the band, the better. When they're playing songs I know the words to, I focus on the lyrics, sing at the top of my lungs, and dance until my back is covered in sweat. It's when I'm not so familiar with the music that my mind wanders and starts thinking about fire or stampedes or gas explosions. Before any concert I check the set list they last played to be ahead of the game.

- Have plenty of water on you. If they don't let you bring water into the venue, head to the bar before you do anything else and get a decent supply. Stay hydrated!

- Bring gum. Super minty gum gives me something to focus on. It also grounds me and snaps me back to reality when dizziness starts to kick in.

- Try not to fight the panic. Be kind to your body—it's not trying to ruin this experience for you. Tell yourself you're going to be OK.

- Put your hands up. You can pretend it's because you're dancing, but secretly you're giving your body a massive stretch, which will help relax your muscles.

- Make sure you're not taking lots of little short breaths. Inhale for three counts, hold for three counts, then exhale for six. You could do this to the beat of the music if it lends itself to it. Disclaimer: I tried this at Blink 182 and it did not work.

- If you're sweating and you have any of that water left, pour some on your head. You'll look really hardcore, trust me.

- Last, don't feel like you have to be in the thick of the crowd. Let your buddies know you like to stand near the exit. Do your own thing. Make sure you're comfortable.

OH WAIT, IT'S NOT JUST ANXIETY...

University signaled the time I learned about anxiety and its effects on my life, but there was more. A few weeks after the GP told me he suspected I had an anxiety disorder, I went back for a checkup and he added one more part to it: "We think you are depressed too."

I've always found depression incredibly hard to describe because it's such a mystery. It exists on its own terms and there's nothing quite like it. What I *do* know is that it made me feel trapped, the same way anxiety makes me feel trapped but heavier, stickier, and more impenetrable. Everything is shrouded in the negative view that I have about myself, my friends, my work, everything. Any moments of joy are short-lived and quickly spoiled by a bitter fluid. While I feel like there's an external pressure, hot and heavy, pressing down on my skull, inside I feel empty and hollow. The only sound I can hear is my own heart beating, taunting me for still being alive.

My depression coexists with anxiety and sometimes the scales tip. When depression takes over, the lights go out. This isn't to say that anxiety is easier to live with, but I have been able to at least attempt productive coping mechanisms when it comes to anxiety. Depression makes that harder. "What's the point of coping mechanisms?" I whisper to myself in a dark room. "I shouldn't really be here anyway."

In my third year of college I became obsessed with the idea of disappearing. I wanted to stop living, but I didn't have the energy to do anything about it. Instead, I'd lie in bed staring at the ceiling and imagine walking for days until atom by atom my body started to vanish. The more I'd walk, the more I'd disappear. I longed to be transparent. No blood or gore. No corpse lying around for someone else to clear up. No one would be too traumatized. I could text everyone saying I'm absolutely fine, I just decided to exit stage left and never come back again. No biggie.

I longed to be transparent.

When anxiety and depression decide to merge and come at me in unison, it's like my body is being moved in two different directions. Anxiety wants me to freak out, panic, run around to get help and call everyone I know, while depression locks my bones in place and tells me to stay put. On the one hand my body is heavy and sluggish; on the other it's whizzing around and unraveling because of the pressure I've put on myself to get it together, be normal, and just get on with things.

Anxiety and depression held hands the day I decided to walk to the top of Bristol's Park street and across to Brandon Hill and sit on the bench made famous by the TV series *Skins*. It was 5 p.m., and no one was there. I imagined most people were in pubs, chatting about their day and weekend plans. I hated myself for being so completely alone in a city with tons of students and a boyfriend I was living with. Why was I *this* lonely? Why did I not make an effort with anyone? Why was I such a loser? I became a detective putting myself under a harsh light trying to get to the bottom of why I was so impossibly alone.

Instead of approaching my predicament with a bit of self-sympathy, I felt angry and ashamed of being me. My anxiety had convinced me that everyone in my class hated me because I was weird and stupid, while my depression told me that they didn't hate me at all—I hated them. I was a judgmental asshole who hated anyone having a good time. I deserved to feel this isolated. I was a bitch.

I looked down at the view below my bench and imagined flinging myself down it. Anyone who knows Bristol knows it's impossible to kill yourself on Brandon Hill; it's not a cliff.

Worst case you'd end up doing a body roll to one of the paths where the road evens out where you'd come to a halt and someone would give you a strange look. It just seemed enticing. To let my body go. To flop it over the hill and roll until I'd stop rolling, and maybe after my brain had rattled around my skull it would snap out of its turmoil.

I tried to summon some extra energy from a pocket of my brain. Something that would get me off this bench, stop fantasizing about tumbling down the hill like a human sausage roll and just go home. Go write something. Go shower. Go talk to someone. Go do something productive. Anxiety whizzed around my head telling me to get off my ass, while depression sat on top of my skull like a helmet that's too tight.

I saw a toddler run down the hill into the arms of her dad. She wore a red bomber jacket and an orange woolly hat and was running down with carefree abandon. She shrieked. Joy made her skin glow. I got up and wiped the frustrated tears that had fallen out of my eyeballs. I steadied my feet, took a deep breath, and exhaled a high-pitched scream while I tried to run without restraint. I ran all the way down the hill. Trying not to worry about tripping. "Just run. Just keep running," I told myself. Then I got to the bottom. I looked behind me. Cabot Tower was staring down at me. The toddler was gaping at

"Just run. Just keep running," I told myself.

me. The dad ushered her away. I left the park and burst out laughing.

This running down the hill incident wasn't some big turning point; I didn't run my way into the sweet arms of recovery. I think what it illustrated was a tiny little turning point, a tiny little injection of life, of weirdness, of wanting to live unashamedly. I've been lucky enough to have a few of these moments. There's been so many times in my life where I'm sitting on a bench or standing on the edge of a platform or lying in a bath clutching a razor blade thinking about how great it would be to extinguish myself. To disappear. And then there's always something, a small feeling, a

tiny spark of electricity that says, "No." It's what walks me to the ER, it's what takes me to my doctor's waiting room, and it's what encourages me to go to therapy and support meetings. That tiny spark makes sure I don't have sharp objects in my room or that I go home when things get too much. That spark keeps me going, and stops me from disappearing completely.

How to find that little spark in your own self when the lights go out:

- Write your thoughts down. It doesn't have to be in full diary form, it can be incoherent or just an angry scribble. This will help keep your mind from running around in circles in its own cage. Set the words free.
- Make a playlist of songs that make you feel something within your whole body; it might be classical, it might be deep house, it might be jazz. I like Bikini Kill and Radiohead and old-school Mariah Carey. I like songs that absorb me, songs I can lose myself in, songs that take me away somewhere else—even if it's just for a moment.
- Stretch your body out. When I stretch I feel good. It doesn't have to be a proper arch your back and lick your asshole type stretch they like to do in yoga, just anything that moves your body in a different way. Feel your body, acknowledge that you have it and it's good to you.

- Go outside. Even if you sit on a bench or on the grass or on a stoop. Go outside. Breathe fresh air.
- Move your body. After you've stretched it, put it into motion. Jump, skip, walk, jog—and ideally scream while you do it.
- Last, remember that you're made up of 70,000,000, 000,000,000,000,000,000,000 atoms. My depression makes me feel small, insignificant, and hollow. I'm not hollow. Not really. I'm filled with organs and skin and mucus and blood that's full of life.

CHAPTER 3

Remember This When You're Scared of Your Own Brain

'I've often felt like I have had no control over my mind. It goes down corridors I don't want it to go. It punishes me, challenges me, and quite frankly, freaks me the fuck out. It's frustrating because my mind lives in my own head, so how can something inside me be working against me in that way?

As a child I often fantasized about drilling a hole in my scalp to let all the bad parts out. Being afraid of my own thoughts is entrapping. It's like walking around with explosives built into your brain but someone else is carrying the trigger. You don't know where they are or when they'll hit the button.

Learning about my brain and what is behind the things that scare me helped me come to terms with my own head. Knowing about the cause and effect of certain symptoms grounds them in biology; they're still annoying and frustrating but I'm not as alarmed.

The first is dissociation. Dissociation is described by the American Psychiatric Association as "a disruption in the usually integrated functions of consciousness, memory, identity, or perception of the environment." It's often a reaction to overpowering stress. For me, it's like my mind folds in on itself. I'm there, but I'm not really there.

There are two strands to dissociation. One is depersonalization, which is often described as a feeling of watching yourself from a distance. The very first therapist I saw as a teenager used to call this "Helicopter Maggy." I'm in a helicopter looking down on whatever it is that I'm doing, often full of judgment and scorn. My school boyfriend used to play in a band, and I'd go to every gig despite the fact that I never knew anyone and hated crowded bars. I'd often stand there and that helicopter would kick in: "Look at that stupid girl, she has no friends, she's so dumb, she can't talk to anyone." I'd then start to tear down everything about myself: my hair, the way I was standing, the way my arms hung loosely next to my body. It meant I could never relax or even enjoy the music. I was my own paparazzi, hovering over myself, putting that horrible self-critical voice on loudspeaker.

The other strand of dissociation is derealization, where you feel disconnected from reality. Often in a high school movie when the protagonist's love interest is seen kissing someone else, time appears to stand still. Shocked, the protagonist watches the horrible events unfold in slow motion. For me, derealization feels like that, only there's no sad indie music playing in the background. I feel spaced out and floaty. People's voices sound far away; mouths appear to move out of sync with sound.

There's lots of reasons why people experience dissociation, from trauma to an inability to process emotional information. Often it's your brain protecting your body from perceived threat. For me, the safest space has always been in my own head. That's where everything takes place. I've always been content sitting by myself playing out conversations and scenarios. Even now, if I need a break from something I'll lie down, shut my eyes, and go somewhere peaceful to mull over my ideas.

While it's natural for me when I feel unsafe to retreat to the place I know best, it's not a very comfortable experience, especially when I have no control over it. I've described it often as having my head trapped in a fishbowl. I can see things, but they're all a bit misshapen and the sounds feel echoey. I want to smash the bowl so badly and be present, but

I can't. The more I think about it, the thicker the glass of the bowl seems to become.

My dissociation has made it difficult for me to always act in a way that I want to, especially in social situations. For example, in a pub meeting a boyfriend's friends for the first time, I want to be outgoing and fun. I want to sound interesting and interested in everything everyone else has to say, when all of a sudden it's impossible for me to string a sentence together. The words that come out of my mouth are all garbled and weird. Why can't I just function normally?

Parts of my self-destructive behaviors have to do with wanting to get out of that fishbowl. I often hope that by causing myself physical or emotional pain, it'll act like someone's chucking a bucket of ice water on me to get me out of a nightmare. I try it with alcohol too. The soft rocking feeling I get after a few large glasses of white wine mimics the weird dreamy feeling of dissociation. They almost mirror each other. It's like I'm sinking into myself but pulling up a chair at the same time. I'm here to stay. It feels nice here.

As well as dissociation, intrusive thoughts that feel more like voices or urges often bombard my brain. Intrusive thoughts are so common that you'd be more of an anomaly if you *didn't* experience them. They're like a little fire you can't put out. They are incredibly persistent and can be quite scary. In the book *Abnormal Psychology: An Integrative Approach*, some of the most common intrusive thoughts are broken down into causing harm to yourself (jumping out of a window) or to someone else (dropping your friend's baby), contamination (catching a disease from a dirty toilet seat), doing something inappropriate (randomly getting up in a meeting to swear at your boss), or safety (thinking you've left the oven on after you leave the house).

For some people, the occurrence and intensity of intrusive thoughts are so powerful you develop your own coping strategies simply to get through the day. The solution to distressing thoughts is never as simple as "just don't think about it"—if only! To prove how impossible it is, social psychologist Daniel Wegner conducted the following experiment. He asked participants to verbalize whatever they were thinking at that very moment for five minutes. The only rule: they had to try their very best not to think about a fluffy white bear. If the white bear did pop into their heads, they had to ring a bell. Despite explicit instructions to avoid thinking about the bear, participants obviously thought about it. In fact, more than once per minute on average.

Similarly, I find the more I tell myself not to think about something, the more I'm likely to think of that very thing. Suppressing my intrusive thoughts only seems to make them thrive. I might be sitting at the back of the bus trying to calm my anxiety down a bit because the bus is busy and fogged up inside from bad weather. I'm just about coping when a little light flickers in my brain that says: "Wouldn't now be *such* a bad time to yell *I've got a bomb*!" And there we have it. Not only am I nervous because the bus is filled to the brim with

humans, I'm now convincing myself that I'm teetering on the edge of madness, coaxing myself to be a pretend terrorist, which will inevitably freak the hell out of these innocent people. I follow the thought all the way through to getting arrested, facing a hearing, losing my job, having my parents be disappointed, and having my boyfriend explain to his friends that his girlfriend is in prison because she thought it would be hilarious to shout *"Bomb"* on a bus. I'd lose everything in an instant. I shouldn't do it. But maybe I should? No. Don't do it. But what *if*?

Feel exhausted yet?

So much of our day is spent being mentally active that we

come to rely on our mind to work the way we want it to. However, sometimes our train of thought goes down an unwanted path conjuring up a reaction that's both unwelcome and perhaps even harmful.

When I'm depressed, every single thing around me becomes a tool to hurt myself with. An impulse tells me to stand closer to the platform, to smash my face into a mirror, to down a whole bottle of bleach or run in front of a car. It's exhausting and it colonizes so much of the good in my life.

I've even had intrusive thoughts creep in right before or during sex. Right as I'm about to come, my brain challenges me to think: "What would be the most inappropriate image to conjure up right now?" Then images will flash—maybe a dead relative, maybe the lady who works in the cafeteria at work—or suddenly I'll begin to recall some of the horrific images I've seen on the news. Then when I finally come I can convince myself I'm an absolute psychopathic nightmare. You come to an image of bloodshed and violence. *You're a freak.*

People with intrusive thoughts, especially people who have OCD, often develop repetitive actions or compulsions to try and stop the intrusions from happening. Compulsions are things you do to try to make the obsessive irrational thoughts go away. Everyone's coping strategies are unique to them, but often compulsions fall under these categories:

- Checking (repeatedly checking the appliances, blood pressure, locks)
- Repeating (rereading the same sentence, writing the same word, tapping)
- Counting (steps, bricks, numbers out loud)
- Washing (ritualized bathing, cleaning, brushing)
- Ordering (books, clothes, dishes)
- Physical (biting nails to line all up, blinking, shrugging)

Depending on where I was in my life, I had different compulsions to manage intrusive thoughts. In college I was living with my boyfriend, P., who I'd come to fully depend on. When I felt him slipping away from me, I became obsessed with the idea that he'd walk out of our flat and die, or even worse, that I might accidentally kill him. The idea of losing him was so painful to me that I couldn't stop thinking about that very thing. I developed weird compulsions and rituals that I felt I had to carry out to make sure he'd be safe. One involved having to kiss him back three times if he ever kissed me on the lips. Some were more sexual, and others had more to do with our flat: how the pillows were positioned and the arrangement of our books and DVDs.

My compulsions were starting to dictate my life and they were causing me to get sucked into a strange, very isolated state where I felt I couldn't live without P. It wasn't some form of romantic desperation, it was larger than me, than us: he was my life support. In my head I couldn't breathe without him. The pressure this put on P. was incredibly unfair. Every time he met up with someone else I took this as an extreme form of rejection, which made it worse. It also meant that I put no faith in myself. I didn't see myself as whole. I was only ever someone's girlfriend, and not a great one at that.

A lot of my intrusive thoughts are visual: they appear as a single image that flashes over and over again. Most often it'll have something to do with the body or something horrific I saw online. I am one of those people who will see a click-bait headline along the lines of "ONLY WATCH THIS CYST VIDEO IF YOU'RE NOT SQUEAMISH," and just to prove the headline wrong, I'll watch it, often with one eye closed. Some I can handle, especially when the headline oversells what's happening on-screen. Others leave me feeling sick. When there's gross itty-bitty things coming out of people's skin, I have to find that part on my own body and rub it at least nine times, making sure there are no itty-bitty things stuck in mine.

Sometimes my visual intrusions make me laugh. I want to shake my head and say: "Come on brain, not now, OK?" But there was a time when these images appeared so often and were so persistent I lived in fear that I was losing my mind. I had one counselor—a very timid, kindhearted Irish woman who worked at my university—who gave me a handy trick. It involved Club Penguin.

In case you've never heard of it, Club Penguin was a multiplayer online game (it got the boot a while back). My younger brother was very into it growing up, and I used to watch what he was up to over his shoulder. There's a bit where you dress up your penguin avatar, which for me was always the best part. You can dress them up in Converse, shades, concert T-shirts, dinosaur costumes, trucker caps, blond wigs—the options are enjoyably endless.

When I was at university I hadn't really thought about Club Penguin in years. At this time my anxiety was hellish, and a medley of panic attacks and intrusive thoughts was becoming an almost hourly occurrence. I completely isolated myself to avoid having these episodes in public.

Freaky creepy-crawlies under my skin hijacked most of my thoughts. I was obsessed. The fear wouldn't leave me alone. It popped up when I was in the shower, making food, reading a book, or on the bus. I stopped being able to look at my own body. I just imagined creepy-crawlies under there. I scratched my skin raw just to make sure there was nothing there, but it didn't help. I'd tell myself to just not think about it, but it made it come back tenfold.

I decided to quarantine myself out of the shame that my brain couldn't let go of this stupid irrational bug fear. I thought if it struck me when I was out or in a lecture or talking to someone in the corridor, I'd probably show it on my face. Maybe I'd feel sick and vomit all over someone. I couldn't let that happen. I had to protect myself from the outside world and protect them from me. One day I had a counseling appointment on a campus that was a ten-minute bus ride away. I knew I had to go. Something cracked a bit in my mind, and I needed help. My self-induced quarantine was not a permanent solution.

I tackled that bus ride like I was heading into war. I armed myself with my tools: water, chewing gum, a book, a French language audiotape, and some crackers. It was in the heat of the summer, which didn't help, but I managed to get a seat by an open window, and the cool breeze felt like an escape route should I need one. I kept switching from book to audiotape to breathing deeply, all the while pushing the bug image down like I was trying to drown it in a puddle. It wouldn't die though. It was testing me.

> I tackled that bus ride like I was heading into war.

Miraculously, I got to my appointment and sat down in a sticky fake-leather chair that was even more uncomfortable now that it was so warm. My counselor asked: "What's been happening to you this week?" I tried to swallow the big ball of shame that was rising up in my throat. I didn't want her to judge me or to think I was properly losing my shit, but I knew I needed to tell someone about my thoughts. I really needed some help.

I told her about the bugs under my skin. We'd been talking about intrusive thoughts before, so the foundation was there for us to be able to discuss it without me grappling for the right words. She asked me to properly describe everything about the image, but as I did so I began to squirm in my chair. I started rubbing my arms and clenching my fists. She told me to stop, and what seemed very out of the blue then said, "Have you ever heard of Club Penguin?" I was zapped out of my discomfort. The randomness of the question threw me, but also instantly reminded me of my brother who lived back home in the Netherlands, and I missed him so much.

"Yes. I mean, I never played it, but my little brother loves that game. I've seen him on it a lot."

"OK, good. Do you remember that bit where you can dress your penguin?"

I knew exactly what she was describing. The brilliant thing about Club Penguin is that its interface is so friendly and bright it easily sticks in your mind. I visualized that part of the game and the little wardrobe that pops up on the side.

My counselor then told me to imagine myself in that image that I found so troubling—bugs crawling everywhere and my skin bursting open from all those critters squirming about. She told me to focus on my arm in particular, but then imagine that arm in Club Penguin mode. Dress the arm up in a funny hat, she said. Put a mustache on it, or an armband, or a cap, or a wedding dress. Part of me was thinking, "What the fuck is this?" and another part obeyed her. My arm detached itself from me, mentally, and fully immersed itself in the game. It wasn't something that was scaring me anymore; it was funny, kinda cute, and totally harmless. I pictured all the little bugs and gave them hats too. I felt less threatened and grossed out.

I wouldn't say this technique is a magical cure. I can't dress up all my anxieties in a pink cowboy hat and suddenly feel great about my life, but particularly for intrusive visual images they help me put my own spin on them, make them less scary. I spend a lot of time on the internet, on forums and threads. Almost every day, I'll see something that makes me go, "*Oh nooo!*" Sometimes it won't affect me, and sometimes it'll stick with me for the whole day, but at least I know it won't ruin my life.

One of my favorite times using the Club Penguin technique was when I was harboring a lot of paranoia about a manager at work who had it in for me. Big chunks of my paranoia were justified: she used to schedule meetings deliberately when I couldn't make them, avoid eye contact with me in group discussions, or say hi to everyone on our bank of desks but me. My anxiety about her trying to fire me escalated into random flashes of her trying to club me to death at work with a hammer (yep, thanks brain for making a shitty situation even shittier). I got up once to make a coffee and I could feel her walking behind me.

My brain quickly conjured up an image of her walking close to me, hammer in hand, about to strike, and it made my heart rate go up. I distanced myself from the image, tried to look at it from above, and turned her body into a massive white marshmallow. Instead of her charging toward me, she was bouncing around the office like a big Jigglypuff. It made me chuckle and I was able to make my coffee in peace (and even manage a courteous hello when our paths crossed).

The difficulty with intrusive thoughts is that the more I try to block them the louder they become. It feels like yelling at an incoming freight train, and every time you yell *stop*, it's only coming in closer. Instead of shouting "Stop!" or "Go away!" I've learned to try to say other things. If, like me, you've been a bit of a sucker for self-help books, you might have come across the saying "This too shall pass." It's a little bit of a cliché, but when you strip all that away, the core of the saying can feel incredibly true in a moment you need it the most. Whatever turmoil you're going through, it's going to be over at some point—nothing is permanent (maybe apart from the blue butterfly tattoo on my forearm). While there might be more turmoil awaiting you around the corner, you'll deal with that when you get there, and once you do, it'll be over too. When I'm struck by an avalanche of negative thinking, I tell myself that it will pass, that it will wash over me, that this state I'm in isn't forever.

This state I'm in isn't forever.

Even stars that seem to live in the sky forever flare up and eventually exhaust their fuel and collapse back into darkness. This probably sounds melancholic, but it reminds me that permanence really is an illusion. My panic attacks make me feel like I'm being burned up. Heat flashes across my body. I get rashy and dizzy, but despite the fact that every time I've

had an attack I've assumed this would be it for me and I'll be trapped in this hell forever, the burning subsides. My eyesight goes back to normal. The heat dies down and I can breathe again. It's so important to hang on to the fact that it's not forever. It will pass, and I will make it out to the other side each time.

Another nifty trick I've adopted to combat panic and intrusive thoughts is to talk back to them; still not to yell "Stop!" but to actually have a bit of a conversation. The voice doing the talking isn't a voice that belongs to me, it's the voice of someone I love, respect, and admire, and it makes me feel eternally calm. That voice is Oprah.

Oprah is a legend and an icon. She is arguably the most

influential and powerful woman in the world, and what makes her so enticing as a voice of reason in my head is that she oozes empathy. In fact, it's part of her show, her persona, and how she's always interacted with guests and audience members. She always felt to me like a badass nurturing grandmother, dishing up chicken soup and life-changing advice at the same time. The version of her that has developed in my head thrives because it listens. Even if my mind is going a hundred miles an hour, the Oprah voice will slow it down and unpick it.

It helps even more if I imagine myself as a guest on her show. When I'm on the London Underground, which is hellishly busy at the best of times, and I can feel that sense of panic starting to rise, I pretend we're talking about what I'm going through. It helps if I speak as someone who has been through it and survived, so instead of going, "*Oprah, OMG this Tube is so busy. Help!*" I'm saying to her, "Yes, I used to really struggle with panic attacks on the Tube, but now I'm OK, I can manage." Being on my own imagined version of her show allows me to visualize myself on the other side. I've been through the panic and I'm out of there now.

If I want to prevent what I think might be a panic-triggering situation, I'll imagine going on her show and talking about something more general. Maybe about how stupid some of my ex-boyfriends are, or how well my movie is doing (it's important to note that fictional me has not only survived panic attacks, she's also got at least five Oscars).

Having Oprah weigh in on my life, even if it's a slightly fictionalized version, is soothing and distracts me from the hordes of tourists flooding the platform at Oxford Circus.

Oprah or Club Penguin, they're both part of my intrusive-thought fight plan. I call on them like Zordon from *Power Rangers* when he gets all their watches beeping and they need to report for duty. Sometimes though, the intrusive-thought fight plan isn't enough. I need a real outside voice that's not just in my own head. While I've always felt proud of being self-sufficient and able to get on with things alone, when I'm stuck in a feedback loop of hell I need someone outside of my body to snip the loop. Sometimes it's with their own opinion, while other times their opinion spawns a different viewpoint in my own head and I'm able to climb out of quicksand.

This outside voice is often my therapist or a good friend. It's important to me that it's someone I trust. The nature of my intrusive thoughts is that they're on repeat. So having someone say, "Don't worry, there are no bugs crawling around your skin," isn't really enough to make them stop. Three minutes later I'm going to have to ask them again, and this might repeat throughout the day. It's key I don't feel ashamed or judged, or that my friend is running out of patience.

The whole nature of a mental feedback loop is that it's tricky to unshackle yourself in one swift swoop. It takes time, and it's always going to want to drag you back in. I might approach a friend with a problem. Even something practical and simple like: I don't know what to do about the fact that my rent is increasing next month. They might help me reach a logical conclusion that I agree with, but one moment later I can feel myself sinking into that same problem. All the different options, scenarios, and potential outcomes swarm around my head like bees. I can see how it might be frustrating for that other person when I'm back to where I was in the beginning of our conversation, but repetition is key. I need to hear their advice more than once. It's like they're tossing me a life preserver when I'm drowning at sea, but it might take a few tries before I'm able to cling on.

A lot of my techniques fall under an idea called mindfulness. Mindfulness belongs to a school of Buddhist meditation. Professor Jon Kabat-Zinn, who founded the MBSR (mindfulness-based stress reduction) program, defines it as a nonjudgmental awareness of the present moment, through focusing attention intentionally on the moment-by-moment experience. For me, this translates to viewing my intrusive thoughts and acknowledging that they're there without getting annoyed, scared, or angry at myself for the fact that they're there. Imagine you're lying in a field looking up at the sky and watching the clouds go by without passing any judgment. The clouds aren't bad or good, they're just clouds. You're seeing them detached from any emotional reaction you might have. You're giving your mind space to view something just as it is without making up your mind immediately.

I once had a big batch of intrusive thoughts break out while I was in the middle of a company-wide meeting. The meeting involved a fancy presentation that thankfully I didn't have to take any part in. The three company bosses were giving a big speech about how much the new sales team had brought in. I was annoyed at myself because there had been free pizza in the middle of the room and I had conveniently sat myself next to it. When people started pouring into the room, they all went for the pizza and huddled in the same position. Soon enough I felt like I was in the middle of an onion and the rings around me were all the other people. I was about to get up to move, but the bosses came in and the talk started. I told myself to stay put so I wouldn't cause a big scene.

As the talk went on, I got more and more panicky. I thought, "What if I really need to pee, what if I need to vomit, what if I need to shit? How will I get up? How will I survive this?" The more I thought about how I couldn't escape the room unnoticed, the more I really wanted to. My thoughts were getting stronger and stronger, and nothing seemed to quiet them. Even Oprah was nowhere to be seen. Instead of suppressing them, I took a deep breath and tried to hear what they were saying.

To be honest, they sounded like a gaggle of irrational children in a supermarket cart: *"Mum, give me that ice cream now!"* I listened though and didn't think about how they were making me feel emotionally. Instead I paid attention to what was happening to me physically. I focused on my stomach, where I felt queasy from anxiety, but nothing indicated I was going to eject stomach bile everywhere as my thoughts were suggesting. I inhaled and filled my body with air. I exhaled, and the nausea subsided a little. I was onto something. I was calmly breathing through the stress. I was noticing what was happening and listening to my thoughts like a helpful bystander or perhaps a scientist observing a simple experiment through a microscope.

When our CEO stopped talking, I realized I'd made it to the end of the presentation. People started filing out of the room. It was 5 p.m. on a Friday, which is akin to it being the last day of school before the summer. Everyone dashed around me and grabbed a free beer from the fridge. I felt I was somewhere else, somewhere better. I was secretly incredibly proud of myself for sitting through the presentation, for sitting with my thoughts. Yes, it was awful, and I did think I was going to hurl for a bit there, but I was able to calm myself down. I felt like I'd just jumped out of a plane and landed safely on the ground: I did it! I was chuffed, I even remember giving myself a little squeeze.

In these situations, you need to give yourself a little mental boost, but it's hard to say, "You go, girl!" to yourself when you don't really believe it. If you're anything like me, you're probably quite allergic to clichés, especially in the style of anything you might see plastered on someone's Instagram with a soft pink background and Moon Flower font. However, sometimes I need a helping hand, and sometimes that helping hand comes in the form of a mantra. So here are some not so cringeworthy (I hope!) mantras that help me when my brain needs to chill the fuck out:

- The battle cry: All right anxiety, we got this. GIVE ME YOUR WORST
- The good advice: Remember you went through this before and you can go through this again
- The distraction: "Look at this stuff . . . Isn't it neat . . . ?" Or sub this for whatever Disney song you know totally by heart. If you find yourself somewhere you can belt it out loud, even better!

GIVE ME YOUR WORST

- The reward: When this is over we're getting pizza
- The Hogwarts chant: Those patient Hufflepuffs are true and unafraid of toil (or whatever your House description is!)
- The football coach speech: Don't try and get over it, walk through it
- Or even better: "Clear eyes, full hearts, can't lose," from *Friday Night Lights* (if you haven't watched this show, definitely do; you'll get a wealth of brand-new motivation!)
- The song from the musical *Avenue Q*: "Everything in life is only for now"
- The mindfulness quote: You can't stop the waves, but you can learn to surf (even though I probably can't because I have no balance, so maybe I'll learn how to body board)
- The badass cheer: Feel the fear and do it anyway. I stole this from Dr. Susan Jeffers' book, which is all about being more assertive.
- The happy memory: Remember that time you were eight and you entered a school talent show on your own and you were so scared you almost peed your pants but you got through it and fucking won!
- The power ballad: "At first I was afraid, I was petrified" and then I fast forward straight to, "I will surviiiive"
- This piece of advice from *Gone with the Wind*: "After all, tomorrow is another day"

■ And last, this less profound piece of advice aimed at my anxiety, not myself: "Shut your fucking face, Uncle Fucka." Thank you, *South Park*!

HOW TO FIND OUT WHAT TRIGGERS YOU

I'm hypersensitive to just about anything. I always imagine my brain to be naked, completely vulnerable to every single stimulus around it. I genuinely don't think it's all bad. I have a *lot* of feelings, some not very useful, but some are fun. Movies become visceral experiences where I'm rooting for the character so much I can completely lose myself. It's also made me a good listener. When someone's telling me a story, I always feel like I'm totally there with them, clinging to their every word. I also feel like I'm quite perceptive. I've often been the first to uncover office gossip just by noticing people's little mannerisms: the slightly tense way they walk out of meeting rooms (yep, they're going to quit), or the two coworkers who always gently nudge each other's shoulders when they walk past each other's desk (definitely banging).

On the negative side, being hypersensitive means a lot of things have the potential to send me into a bad spell: a particular song, a word, a shrug, an item of food. A little blip can make me redefine my great day to *"Why the fuck did I bother to get up?"* When I think about triggers, it feels like there are too many to name. I've thought about encasing myself in a bubble, like Bubble Boy, but instead of protecting myself against germs, I'm protecting myself against triggers.

Someone once told me a story about a camel in London Zoo (hang in there, this is relevant). Every day this camel goes for a guided walk around the zoo so guests can enjoy seeing it up close. Before the camel goes for a walk, one of the other zookeepers goes ahead and makes sure that the route is as close to what the route looked like the day before as possible. If there's an overflowing trash can, it'll be removed. If there's an umbrella bopping around that's too bright, the owner will be asked to put it down. Basically, if the camel sees anything that's too out of the ordinary it'll freak out. Everything needs to be the same.

I can relate to this camel. While it would be super boring, life as a simple and safe routine that I can repeat over and over means I'd be free from triggers. I wouldn't self-harm or experience bouts of rage or misery. Thing is, life really isn't like this, and for good reason. Your experiences are often muddy and complicated and subject to random changes and challenges. The best way to avoid triggers is to figure out what they actually are. What makes me feel uncomfortable and what drives me to the edge?

> The best way to avoid triggers is to figure out what they actually are.

I need to see things laid out in front of me to have them sink into my brain. I was a visual learner in school. I had to plaster math equations and history facts on my walls to be able to memorize them. If this strikes a chord with you, you might find having some sort of visual account of your moods very helpful. Long live the journal!

"Journaling" is a bit of a trendy buzzword, but the act of keeping a diary dates from the second century. Type "bullet journal" into a search engine and you'll see how many people are reaping its benefits. In simple terms, this is a handy organization system with a set of signs and signals that you can decide on and use how you want. It's a mix between a to-do list, notebook, and diary and essentially helps you manage your time. On top of this you can use it to track your thoughts, moods, activities, big events, small events, tasks, deadlines, and how these might all feed into your mental and physical health.

I struggled a bit with returning to diary writing because it reminded me so much of being an angsty teen, scribbling down overly emotional poetry, declaring my love for some guy who sat behind me in class. However, I've come to see journaling as something that's very grown-up, sensible, and ultimately very useful.

The thing I've enjoyed the most about journaling is that it's like a social media platform but for myself (so it's an antisocial platform). I use it both to look forward and to look back. I'll make my weekly plan, but I'll also stick in theater tickets or quotes or lyrics from songs I've been enjoying. My journal is a scrapbook of all the things that have made me feel good and a planner for all the things I'll do to carry on that feeling.

There are lots of different methods to tackling the organizational part to bullet journaling. Don't fall into the trap of having to make it look "pretty." There's loads of Instagram accounts dedicated to all the intricate doodles people do in their journals: little symmetrical check boxes and stunningly drawn banners. Thing is, no one is going to see your journal (unless you want them to), so who cares what it looks like? It just has to make sense to you, that's all.

Journaling has helped me to slow my life down a level. When I feel like I'm in the center of a whirlpool, and life is the water thrashing around and around, stepping back makes it calm down for a bit. Jotting down my problems, what I need to tackle, and what needs my immediate attention makes everything more manageable.

> Journaling has helped me to slow my life down a level.

I also found a lot of value in tracking moods so I can start to think about what might be causing some of them. I give my day a number out of ten for tiredness, sadness, anger, etc. To no one's surprise, PMS causes a lot of those numbers to go up, but apart from that I found that while I *had* cut down drinking, I hadn't really cut down enough. I was still drinking more than a bottle of wine three times a week, which was making me wake up miserable. I wasn't sleeping enough, and every time I met up with my boyfriend I'd end up stressed out and frustrated. I needed to make some big life adjustments, but I was too stuck in the middle to see exactly what needed to change.

If you feel tracking, scrapbooking, and journaling is something you might like to try, you should splurge on a bitchin' diary. If it's not colorful or "you" enough, customize it with wrapping paper or magazine clippings. Make this space totally yours. Mine is as garish and weird looking as my MySpace page was in 2005, and that's exactly how I like it.

KEEP TRACK OF WHAT MAKES YOU FEEL GOOD

Instead of just thinking about what makes me miserable, I started tracking the little everyday things that boost my mood. If I'm at work—which, let's face it, we all are most of the time—and I can feel the pull of self-doubt, I make sure I leave my desk to go out for lunch. Perhaps I'll read my book under a tree, or go for a little walk. If I have enough time I'll make myself a quick playlist of angsty folk songs.

To help you discover what your little pick-me-ups might be, try to make a note of them. Think of it like you're assembling a tool kit; once you've experienced something that acted as a little mood booster, add it to the kit. You can use it when things take a bad turn.

Sometimes your tool kit is going to work wonders, other times it might not. Unfortunately, when I'm in a bad mood because I've had to pay a shitty tax bill, I'm not necessarily going to feel better because I read my book for a bit. Some things are just universal mood killers. Despite that, having a collection of options to turn to when I'm lost or adrift is comforting. I've made a list of some of these things below. I hope they might inspire you to list some of your own:

- Finding a band I'd never heard of before on Spotify and being blown away
- Bonus points if they happen to be playing in town soon
- Showing a friend a great pic I took of them, and for a second they actually see themselves as the wonderful ray of sunshine and beauty that I see them as
- Even better when they make that photo their new profile pic
- Waking up early on the weekend just to lie in bed and enjoy all the time I still have left to sleep
- Giving a bunch of unworn clothes to the charity shop and feeling like I've shed a lot of excess skin
- Rescuing a seemingly dead plant in my bedroom and giving it a new lease on life
- Reading a really dense and wordy article in a scientific journal but actually sort of getting it

- Running for the bus, making it, and not feeling like death on a stick because I haven't been smoking as much that week
- Bonus when the bus driver smiles in a way that says "congrats," but also "don't worry, would've waited for you anyway"
- Going for a brisk walk in the winter and feeling the cold air rush in and out of me like it's purifying my lungs
- Walking home after a yoga class when my shoulder stand was maybe 3 percent better than it was last time
- Catching someone's eye when it's weird chanty time in that yoga class and you both laugh
- Listening to a song that's so good I have to walk around the block because I need to listen to it again before I get home
- Going home to find I actually made my bed for once and it looks really cozy and inviting
- Discovering a quiet corner of my office building that's not as busy
- Making someone laugh so much a little tear forms in the corner of their eye
- Laughing so much I'm not omitting any sounds, just sort of doubling over slapping my thigh
- Sharing a problem with someone and feeling that bit of pressure lift off my chest
- Waking up and drinking in the smell of someone next to me who I love even though I'm very jealous they're still asleep

- Waking up in a bed by myself and starfishing my heart out
- Looking at old family photographs and laughing at my old haircuts
- Randomly treating myself to a fancy shower gel or flowers or silky underpants
- Opening a fresh notebook and feeling like everything is possible
- Going to a big social event and finding that one person I happen to totally connect with
- Going to the pub after a long, strenuous hike
- Getting drenched outside and diving straight into bed with a fresh set of PJs when I get home
- Also, getting into bed when I've put fresh sheets on
- Finding that perfect laundry detergent that makes everything smell like a meadow
- Making a salad that's both healthy and also miraculously sort of tastes OK
- And then eating a dessert after because I just had salad
- Spending a chunk of time with someone who I expect is about to leave and then they suggest staying out a bit longer
- Finding something totally random in a gift shop that I just have to get for someone
- Leaving myself enough time to get a fancy coffee before I get to my desk

- Also being the first one in so I get to revel in that calm before the storm
- Feeling a gentle ache in my muscles from doing something that didn't feel like exercise at all (e.g., helping someone move, or going for a bike ride, or jumping into a pond)

CHAPTER 4

Remember This When You Want to Hurt Yourself

Sometimes my head gets so tangled up I resort to inflicting physical pain on myself in the hopes of making some sense of it all. When I was sixteen, I self-harmed for the first time. It felt like I'd opened up a door that would never get shut again. I felt the brief endorphin rush as I broke my skin and red liquid trickled across my thigh. The rush was almost instantly replaced by fear. I felt extremely scared because I couldn't quite believe what I'd done. I crawled into bed and tried to make sense of the situation, but my brain was zigzagging through my skull. I couldn't rationalize my actions.

Through my fast and shallow breathing I could hear the soft voices of my parents in the living room. My brain was caught up in a tennis match between two urges: go out there and ask for help, or stop crying, go to sleep, and put a bandage on your arm (no one needs to know what you've done).

I wanted to choose the first option. I imagined what it would be like to walk into the living room and whisper, "Help." My dad's eyes would widen the way they do when he's worried. My mum would lunge toward me and hug me. They'd get me a bandage and make me some tea. That part seemed easy. I could do that. Then came the tough bit. I would drink the tea and put my mug down. My dad would ask why I'm so upset. My mum would ask what happened to my arm, and I knew that's when my throat would close up and block my voice from coming out. It seemed too painful, too awkward, too big a task. Instead I shut my eyes, wrapped an old Euro Disney T-shirt around my wrist, and went to sleep.

I often think about that moment. If only I'd nudged myself out of bed and into the living room. That moment became a pattern that repeated itself over and over. I have an urge to ask someone to help me—a counselor, a boyfriend, a housemate, or a friend—but instead I feel like I can't. This is my dirty secret and I should just get on with it. No one can help me, no one wants to help me.

Self-harm quickly became a crutch for me to manage the cacophony of negative voices whizzing around my head. In part because teenage me didn't know anxiety and depression were a thing. Self-harm helped me manage my symptoms, just in the worst way possible.

> Self-harm helped me manage my symptoms, just in the worst way possible.

For me, self-harm feels like I'm standing on a bridge and the wind is so extreme it can blow me away at any moment, and then I find a little trapdoor that leads me down below, to another bridge where there's no wind and I can just move forward freely. Self-harm is that trapdoor.

Reasons why I've self-harmed in the past:

- I'm angry but the anger refuses to leave my body
- I'm struggling to be present, to be in my body, and I need something to ground myself
- I'd rather be in physical pain than deal with emotional pain
- I'm desperately trying to find something that will zap me out of my zombie brain
- I'm upset about something but I can't quite put my finger on it, and if I don't do something now it will swallow me whole
- I have disappointed myself so irreversibly I have to physically punish myself

- I have had too much to drink and it just seems like a completely logical thing to do
- I watched something on my laptop that triggered a flashback to something I need to expel from my brain
- I feel like my voice isn't being heard and it has nowhere to go but scream angry red lines out onto my body
- I've not self-harmed in years and I can finally be in a place where I can get away with it because there's no one watching over me, and like a naughty kid I give in to the urge
- I see all the scars that already sit on my arm and it makes me sad and ashamed and hate myself, and so I think, "Fuck it, what's one more going to do?"

Reasons I definitely haven't self-harmed, despite what some people assume:

- I'm desperate for attention
- I've been listening to My Chemical Romance all day
- I'm doing it out of spite
- I'm doing it to piss off my parents
- I'm weak
- I want people to feel sorry for me
- I'm showing off
- I'm addicted to the endorphins
- I'm being dramatic
- I'm overly sensitive
- I'm doing it to manipulate someone else

- I like blood
- I like creating problems for myself

I became extremely adept at hurting myself, using many methods. Before going to sleep with my bloody arm wrapped in toilet paper, I'd set myself little reminders in the form of Post-it notes: "Get help," "Tell Mum," "Talk to *someone!*" Then morning would come and I'd gather these bits of paper in a hurry, embarrassed at how desperate they all sounded.

As a teenager, when my self-harm scars became noticeable, my mum enforced a "no sharp objects" rule in my room. All the scissors, razors, and tweezers were removed. This helped for a bit. While it annoyed me, I knew the inevitable confrontation that would arise if I protested would be far worse. Having my mum's beady eyes scan my limbs each morning felt intrusive, but it did stop me harming for a few months, which felt long at the time.

Over the years, there's been only one other person who stopped my harming: P., my first boyfriend. The wounds that blossomed on my forearms upset him, and the guilt I felt looking at his face each time he'd spotted one outweighed any relief I was getting out of it. His life at this point wasn't exactly smooth sailing. He had a manic-depressive parent he often had to track down in the middle of the night. I didn't want to be an addition to his escalating list of worries. I decided I'd stop. My intentions were good, but once again I didn't stop harming for me; it was in someone else's interest.

Slowly but surely I found other ways to get back into my habit.

At age twenty-six, my self-harm spiraled dangerously out of control. Between the first time I self-harmed at sixteen and then, I'd seen six counselors. I'd been on meds for five years. I'd stopped harming on and off for periods of time but I hadn't been able to quit completely.

It was a mild March evening. I was heartbroken and sad about how my life had derailed. Anything productive and helpful I'd learned thanks to counseling and research I'd tossed aside. I was standing outside a pub in Stoke New-ington with a lit cigarette in hand, causing myself injuries that would require weekly visits to the ER for the next few months.

Inside were five friends; we were celebrating one of their birthdays. The evening was jolly. Someone I was getting to know better romantically was there too. Possibilities were in the air. Good things could have happened if I'd had less to drink, if I hadn't gone outside on my own, if I'd asked some-one for help, if if if.

My life at this point was shrouded in the aftermath of yet another relationship coming to an end, which meant I was constantly going back and forth between our old shared flat and my new room, loaded with boxes and crates and a torn-apart heart. And yet I had woken up that day feeling uncharacteristically optimistic. Today was the last trip I had to make and I felt relieved. This would mean the end of living in the in-between: I could finally start afresh. To make a celebratory morning out of it, I treated myself to brunch in my old neighborhood: French toast with Greek yogurt and peaches. I invited my friend who lived around the corner. I wanted him to celebrate with me. I felt proud that I reclaimed my old brunch spot and that I could still enjoy things. Old things could feel new. I could do this.

Just as we'd placed our orders, the universe decided to become a badly scripted romantic comedy: in walked my ex-boyfriend. I knew this by how drained of blood my friend's face had become. My ex hadn't walked in alone; he was there with a woman. Blond, sequin top, and a bright pink miniskirt.

My ex and his breakfast partner had their backs to us, so the most sensible option was to get through our breakfast (quickly), pay, and then go (hopefully unnoticed). We ate our food in utter silence, like we were two kids playing hide-and-seek, wanting to remain hidden until an adult called us to safety. My friend let me walk out first and joined after. When we made it out into the fresh spring air we both exhaled a breath we'd been keeping in for half an hour.

A near hysterical laugh rose up out of me and filled the empty street. I bent over to catch my breath; all this nervous energy was spilling out. I couldn't stop laughing. I tried to compose myself so we could keep walking. We walked to Clissold Park, where we went around in circles dodging kids on tricycles. The grass was thick and heavy with spring. It was a beautiful day, which only seemed to mock the shit situation we'd just left behind. Despite all this, I was still chuckling. I think it was easier to find the whole thing funny than to admit how terrible it really felt. Instead, I focused on how unlikely it all was, how hilariously cruel the universe must be. My friend joined me in my laughter, albeit somewhat apprehensively. I then stopped and decided to voice the most superficial thought I was having underneath all that laughter: "She's prettier than me, isn't she?" My friend assured me she wasn't, not that it mattered. We then began to tear her down in a way that was entirely unfair and cruel, and it didn't make me feel better. I told my friend I was ready to go home; screw getting my things at my old flat. I needed to go back to bed.

"I'm not leaving you on your own."

"No, it's fine, I'll be OK."

"Still, I'm not leaving you."

On his insistence, we ventured into my new neighborhood and watched a Ryan Gosling film at the local Picturehouse cinema. The handsome lead was getting the girl, the bad guys were getting shot, and all I could think about was how utterly pointless relationships were for me. My three years with my ex weren't as meaningful as I'd thought. Within the space of a few days our history had been reduced to an empty flat with tragic bits of Blu Tack where photos once lived. He'd already moved on. He was bringing girls home. I was completely replaceable.

After wasting fifteen pounds on a ticket for a film I was paying zero attention to, I decided to push my dark thoughts away. You know in a cartoon when a character has a nightmare and they shake their head, dispelling the nightmare from their body? That's what I was doing. I kept thinking, "Just get to the end of the day. There's a party in a pub. You can drink then. Just get to the pub. You'll be fine."

At the pub I played the part of happy friend. I smiled, I laughed on cue, and I sat up straight with my hands neatly folded in my lap like a bunch of flowers. My movements were so precise, so calculated, that they were telltale signs that things weren't really OK.

I stopped talking to anyone. I was no longer contributing my own bits of conversation. I was nodding along, feigning attention. I always found that if you nod and narrow your eyes ever so slightly, people are under the impression you're listening to them. I didn't want to listen. I didn't want to be there. My brain had made its decision for me. I wanted to stop hurting, so I needed to go out and hurt myself.

"Off for a smoke," I announced.

"Fancy some company out there?"

"No, I'll be fine. Be right back."

Once outside I lit my cigarette, and I knew immediately I wasn't going to smoke it. I'd wanted to cut myself all day, but under the watchful eye of my friend I'd been unable to. I didn't have anything sharp in my wallet; I must have thrown out my "tools" the last time I promised myself I'd stop harming. At this point my brain was like an overpacked suitcase about to burst. I needed an outlet; I needed some relief. All I had was my cigarette.

I walked over to a big black trash can and stood behind it. I was hidden away from a table full of smokers. I felt like an addict about to take a hit. I could get away with harming if I stayed here. No one would try to stop me.

There was too much wine in my system for me to put my self-harm urge on hold. Desolate heartbreak had anchored itself in me. I held the cigarette to my skin. I felt a dull ache in my forearm, but it wasn't enough. I moved the cigarette up my arm and dug it in deeper, longer. I stared out at the cars whizzing past me. This wasn't enough, I needed more. I did it again and again until my cigarette burned out.

I put my cardigan on and walked back inside the pub on autopilot. I did feel better, sort of. I felt powerful and in control. I felt like I'd done the one thing I'd wanted to do all day: I punished myself and it felt good. After a few more sips of wine, I thought: "All right, round one complete, off for more." I repeated the process again. I left the cigarette on my skin even longer. Vicious thoughts entered my head like a drill bit. They were overpowering. They told me I deserved this. They told me I'd ruined a perfectly good relationship. They told me it was no wonder he'd moved on already considering how much of a shitbag girlfriend I was. I melted myself down with cruel, judgmental thoughts and slid what was left of me into the cracks in the pavement. My cigarette was done. I went back inside the pub, finished my wine, and thought about going outside again. Only I'd used my last cigarette, I didn't have any more.

"Are you OK?" my friend asked.

My head nodded a confident yes, but from inside a tiny voice crawled out of my mouth. A voice that was scared and afraid and knew what I'd been doing wasn't OK. My throat opened up just a tiny bit, just enough to let one word out: "Help."

I stayed the night at my friend's house and left a trail of blood and pus on his white sheets. My arm looked like antidrug propaganda: Watch What Happens When You Shoot Heroin into Your Arm.

I took myself to the ER the next day. My arm was covered in seeping wounds that were starting to yellow. I went up to the reception desk and whispered something about burn wounds and they told me to take a seat. I looked around at the other patients and tried to play a game of Guess Why They're Here. There was a twisted ankle, perhaps a kidney infection, and someone who had something stuck in their eye. When it was my turn to be seen I'd completely forgotten the speech I'd composed for myself about how I'd gotten these injuries. The excuses had fallen away.

"Did someone do these to you?"

"No."

"How did you get them?"

"I did them to myself."

"All right, let's take a proper look."

While the nurse attended to my arms, I sent myself into a guilt spin: "Look at all those hospital resources they're wasting on you, not to mention their time—everyone knows how understaffed the NHS are! You're a burden to society!"

My guilt trip came to a sudden halt thanks to a sharp pain in my arm that shot down to my wrist. The triage nurse was trying to establish whether I'd burned my nerves. Bits of my wound seemed to be devoid of feeling, but the parts that weren't hurt like hell. My nerves were fine, thanks.

Eventually she wrapped my arm up like a really shitty Christmas present and gave me a bandage sleeve to cover my entire arm. She handed me a list of cleaning instructions and I had to promise I'd come back three times a week for the next couple of weeks so they could dress the wound. I followed her rules diligently. For someone who showered about three times a week and lived off cans of sweetcorn and salt-and-vinegar Pringles, I was determined to do this the right way. I followed her rules and treated my body like a friend who needed help rather than my enemy.

Despite my best intentions, when I came back to the same nurse on my third week she didn't look pleased. The wounds had refused to heal. Fluid was still leaking out everywhere. I was referred to a burn clinic in a hospital in Chelsea, and the nurse hoped the specialists would know what to do.

When I walked through the bright white big streets of

south London I felt so alien among the beautiful rows of houses. I shuffled past Instagrammable coffee shops and young mothers juggling chubby babies and yoga mats. I decided I'd have one cigarette on my way there and one on the way back to reward myself. The irony of smoking while my arm was covered in third-degree burns felt like a secret rebellion. The fuckers weren't healing anyway.

The hospital itself was massive and overwhelming. It smelled of antiseptic cleansers. The bright light bounced off the white tiles into my eyes. Plastic flowers dotted the walls and guided me to an empty reception desk. This felt like a good excuse to leave, as no one was there to tell me where to go, until a big green sign ruined my chance of escape. I followed the arrows pointing to the Burns Unit. In my head I imagined this big smoky furnace where people would be crawling around the floor, their skin crispy and charred. Obviously, it's nothing like that at all. The unit was sterile and clinical. Everyone in the waiting room was like me: upright, but with some part of their body wrapped in gauze.

I was ushered into a room by an Irish lady who looked so huggable I wanted to disappear into her soft arms. She sat me down and began inspecting my wounds. "How did you do these?" When I told her what had happened, I added a meek "sorry" at the end. She told me I didn't have to apologize: "My daughter does that." I didn't know if she meant the self-harm or the apologizing, but I nodded like I'd known her daughter for years.

The room filled up with more nurses. They each inspected my arm and poked the wounds. I felt my stomach lurch, my sight became blotchy, and I forced my focus onto their chatter to stifle the panic that was rising inside my body. The nurses were teasing each other about who put the most sugar in their tea. I focused again on the words, the sound of their laughter. I pretended I was at the hairdresser's getting lost in the chatter of friendly women having their hair done. As they nattered away and rustled their plastic aprons, I christened these women my three fairy godmothers. But instead of getting me ready for the ball, they were patching me up to go out there and face the real world again.

Being in that hospital room, handing over my broken body to other people, made me realize it was the first time I'd let other people take care of me. They were scrubbing me clean, tearing bits of scabs and dead skin off, and filling the holes in my arm with antiseptic and honey. They made me promise I'd come back the following week.

I wish I could say that night outside the pub was my final harming episode. It wasn't. Self-harm has been my coping mechanism for more than ten years. It's as natural to me as sneezing or brushing my teeth. I've normalized it in my head, so when I feel the need I just do it: "Why not? What's the big deal?" What I have learned is that it is a big deal because my body deserves better. The latticework of scars on my skin tells me I hate my body, I don't respect it, it's a war zone. Self-love is a term everyone throws around like it's fluffy and easy, but it's actually one of the hardest things you can do—to go through something and accept it rather than work it out on the battlefield of your body.

Things you could do instead of self-harm:

- Tell someone near you that you need them to distract you—you don't have to tell them why. I once made my friend, a die-hard Bon Jovi fan, list all his favorite Bon Jovi songs in order. I closed my eyes and submerged myself in his enthusiasm and the words of each title. It worked (thanks, Bon Jovi!)
- Get a pen and a scrap piece of paper and scribble as hard and fast as you can
- Type out your thoughts on your phone. Don't stop typing until you've let it all out (I have a dozen notes on my iPhone that just say FUCKUFKCUFKCUFCK over and over again)
- Buy a pot of slime from a toy shop and roll and stretch and poke the goo between your fingers
- Bake something that requires paying close attention to step-by-step instructions
- Get up and run, really fast. Don't stop until your heart is leaping up to your throat
- Scream into a pillow (sometimes I make a pillow sandwich with two pillows and my head in the middle)
- Have a warm shower and shock your system with a sudden rush of cold water

- Put on your favorite music from when you were a teen and sing along really, really loudly (any Fall Out Boy song does the trick for me)
- Find a dog, any dog, and pet the dog
- Dye your hair
- Cut your toenails
- Pop three big pieces of bubble gum into your mouth
- Blow up a balloon and then pop it
- Reorganize your wardrobe
- Watch a film you can pretty much quote along with: *Superbad* does it for me
- Doodle your dream house
- Download *The Sims*
- Sign yourself up for a bunch of exercise classes in the near future
- Rub an ice cube over your wrist
- Paint a delicate flower on your skin
- Follow a lot of tattoo artists on Instagram and rank your favorite pieces
- Organize your bookcase by color
- Come up with a new signature in case you become world famous
- Make a playlist for someone
- Phone a friend
- Do a beauty tutorial on YouTube
- Bang your hands loudly on a piano
- Or actually play the piano if you can

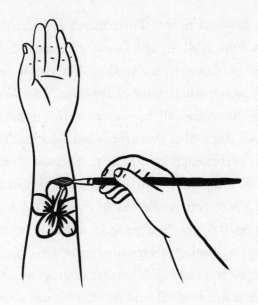

- Watch a shark documentary
- Record yourself voicing all your anger, but do it in Snapchat so you can add a funny filter and make your voice sound like a cute raccoon

Most self-harmers can recall a time someone said something awful about their scars. Special shout-out to the man who stopped in his tracks to yell: "Fucking hell! Did you fall into a cactus?" at me. Or that guy from university who went for: "Whoa, were you mauled by a tiger?" Those are the kinds of reactions that make you want to stay inside and wrap your whole body in a massive plaster for the rest of your life.

When I see self-harm scars on other people, a sequence of

reactions happens to me. First, there's physical sensation: dizziness, nausea, all the usual anxiety ailments. It feels like I'm being confronted with something I didn't ask for; someone else's pain reminding me of my own: "You do this too, you know? Remember all those times you filled the sink with your blood? Remember those times you went too far?" Then there's the overwhelming worry for that person: "God, I hope they're OK," combined with an invisible link that binds us together. We're two people out in the world doing things we're expected to do, like going to school or work, doing some shopping, eating in a restaurant, but we've both clearly, in private, succumbed to this horribly destructive act. Should we exchange numbers? Should we hug? Should we run away from each other?

I'm always fascinated by other people's scars that aren't self-inflicted. I love hearing the stories about battle wounds. Scars are a record of someone's journey thus far. They're souvenirs your body insists on clinging on to. I've tried to see my own scars this way. Just because the stories are sad doesn't mean I have to dismiss them. My scars are a testament to the fact that I somehow made it out the other end time and again.

I don't worry about covering up scars. On a bad day I see them as angry red rosettes, awarded to me for having achieved the highest level of fucking up. On a good day, however, I see them as a testament to my survival. I interviewed Ruby Wax for BuzzFeed about her book *Frazzled*. I told her how all her mental health campaigning had meant a lot to me, and she asked if it was OK to ask what kind of mental health problems I'd experienced. I told her my story, and she looked at my arms and said: "You're very brave for not covering up." After the interview, I walked around Kensington Gardens, and for the first time I felt that maybe I am a bit brave.

I do it so it feels like hell.
—Sylvia Plath, *Lady Lazarus*

Alcohol abuse is another way you can hurt yourself. It's not always as visible as cigarette burns or cuts and bruises, but it can be just as damaging. Drinking with the intent of doing damage is serious. For me, it was born out of self-loathing and the hope of finding some release. You're probably not using alcohol to self-harm when you're drinking in the park with your friends on a Friday night. You do it to self-harm when you get up at 7 a.m., before your parents go to work, adding an obscene amount of whiskey to your cola. You do it to self-harm when you're hiding cans of beer under your bed to drink through the night. You do it when you mix all the alcohol you can find in the kitchen in a bottle, shake it, and genuinely believe that by the time you finish the whole bottle you will feel better. Instead, you vomit and you go to bed feeling nauseated and drowsy and gross.

My teenage binge drinking ironically subsided as soon as it was legal for me to drink. When I went to college and I could technically drink myself into blackout oblivion, I stayed away from alcohol. When I was a student, alcohol became associated with being social, having friends, and having fun. I had neither of those things, and I feared alcohol because it seemed to represent a life I wouldn't be able to have. Plagued with panic attacks, I was so scared of my own brain that I didn't want to experiment with drugs either. I was barely keeping it together sober; what would my brain do to me if I added more chemicals to it?

After college, things changed between alcohol and me. That side of me that existed as a teenager returned. I wanted wine to comfort me, beer to get me through a tough day, and shots to drown out whatever I was worrying about at the time.

I wanted alcohol to submerge me completely, to turn off the lights. I wanted alcohol to make me cooler, more interesting. I wanted alcohol to replace the parts of me I hated with a more fun, sociable version of myself. Sometimes this worked. I evolved into a chattier, dancier version of me. Sometimes it did the opposite. I became even more down, even harder on myself.

A Letter to Sauvignon Blanc

Dear Sauv,

Can I call you Sauv? I think yes. I mean, we've known each other long enough.

On that note, I know I need to see you less. Don't roll your eyes. I know I've said this many times before, but I'm serious.

Do you remember when we first met? I was twelve, finding out which form of self-destruction would fit best. I was testing the limits of my body, what I could handle and what I couldn't. Sometimes I'd bang my head against a wall until it bled. Sometimes I'd etch angry red lines into my thighs with safety pins. Sometimes I'd eat a jar of peanut butter and puke it back up. And then I met you. You were another way to test myself. I used to sneak you into water bottles and pretend you were apple juice. I'd drink you until my stomach felt a pang and then I'd stop, close my eyes, and blink the dizziness away.

The first time I got drunk wasn't in a park with friends. There wasn't a boy I fancied. I didn't impress anyone. Instead, I was alone in bed, clutching my belly, trying to read an *Adventures of Tintin* book while the blurry words bled into the illustrations. When my mum's friend came to check on me one afternoon, I thought, "Shit, I'm busted." Then I had a brilliant idea. "It's my period," I groaned. She left the room and came back with a water bottle and stroked my head. It would be four years before I'd get my first period. I felt pretty smart.

Sauv, I wish I'd spent a little less time with you growing up—twelve was too young. All those stomachaches were futile, they never warned me away from you. I sought you out in all your forms: sharp, yellow, smooth, and cold. Time and time again. You have this eerie ability to slow everything down. It's wonderful, but it's haunting. You're a depressant. You mess up my already muddied levels of serotonin. You confuse cells—those well-meaning cells that take care of mood, desire, and appetite. In your hands they get swirled around like a frustrated painter messing up his palette. You mix everything into a shade of blackout gray.

I don't mean to say you always make me feel sad. Sometimes you make me feel invincible, sexy. You also bring me comfort, a dilatory calm. Coming home after a shit day, you rejig my thoughts. When I'm cold and dizzy from Oxford Street's congested pavements, you warm me up. You make loneliness appealing. You joggle me out of the numbness of everyday existence. You make me feel, even if those feelings are slightly skewed. You crawl into my blood, wrap your spindly fingers around my thoughts, and without warning, yank them right out of me. "Go over there! Go do that! Go feel that! Go exist!" I can hear you roar into the echo chamber. Sometimes you sound like a cheerleader who just snorted her best friend's Ritalin.

The first glass of you always feels like magic. The second feels more settled, more familiar, and the third is almost automatic, a routine. I'm not even excited about it. I approach the barman like I'm approaching my husband in a marriage that's passed its expiration date. We're both there to perform a task. We know what we want, we go through the process; we exchange goods, rinse, and repeat.

I talk a big game when I'm drunk, but one I always find myself apologizing for. I've had to say sorry for kissing somebody else's boyfriend, for punching a man who was just trying to get me home safe, and for vomiting in my own mouth so I wouldn't ruin the taxi driver's car (this plan was going great until I sneezed).

I've consumed you in a melancholy, quiet way too, that night I was maid of honor. I smiled away the feeling that I'd never be good enough to be part of this wedding, took a sip of you, and picked at the Mr. & Mrs. Merlot label, collecting a little confetti heap beneath my hands.

What I mean to say with all of this is that I want to break up with

I want to break up with you, Sauv, just for a little bit.

you, Sauv, just for a little bit. Don't take it the wrong way. I'm
sure we'll see each other soon. I just need a bit of space. My
brain needs some space.

Love,
Maggy

The problem with alcohol is that it stuffs my head with lies.
It makes me lose sight of where I am and what I'm doing.
With alcohol in my blood, I say yes to anything. I'll wander
anywhere. I lose track of what's dangerous and what isn't. On
top of that, my medication means it can be dangerous to add
alcohol to my system, as I'm prone to blacking out. It's a
strange type of unconsciousness where my body is still moving but my mind is completely shut. I'll wake up the next day
to thousands of Facebook messages I fired off in my drunken
haze, or I'll find myself in a strange room with a flurry of
bruises dotted around my ribs.

Alcohol seems like a comforting friend, but alcohol doesn't
tell me the truth.

Alcohol tells me I'm invincible.

Alcohol transforms every person in the bar into a vessel
for me to escape in.

Alcohol tells me that it's OK to hurt myself.

Alcohol tells me that it feels good to hurt myself.

Alcohol tells me I need more
drugs

sex

everything.

Alcohol tells me no one really loves me.

Alcohol tells me I'm going to die soon.

Alcohol tells me the only thing I have to offer is my body.

Alcohol tells me my life is a badly scripted film someone else has written.

Alcohol tells me the only way out is pain.

Alcohol tells me the only way out is the darkness of a blackout.

CHAPTER 5

Remember This
When You Can't Stand
Your Own Body

I have waged a constant battle with my own shape. I've often seen my body as flabby, shapeless, a bit bloblike. What seemed to instigate my attitude toward my body was the very late arrival of puberty that descended upon me like an unwanted guest. I didn't get a period until I was seventeen, and it felt like not only was my uterus spitting out blood, but volcanoes erupted on my chest overnight. My flat butt developed into two big pillowy mounds. There was hair everywhere, and the tufts under my pits carried a sour odor with them. A foreign entity was taking over my body. I was being pushed out, evicted. It was saying: this isn't yours anymore, this belongs to someone else.

I'd squeeze and pinch and poke my own flesh. I wanted to fight back. I dreamed of getting a knife and slicing off my new lumps and curves. I'd sit in the bath and lean to one side, clutching all the flesh that collected. Why couldn't I just remove it? Why was it there? What had I done?

I found it was much harder to hide in my new body. Men stared harder and longer. I walked with my arms across my chest to stop my breasts from bouncing. I tucked my butt in when I was walking so it wouldn't invite anyone to touch it.

I experimented with different clothing styles to try and reclaim my identity that my breasts had taken away from me. I wasn't curvy and feminine; that just didn't suit me. Instead I tried to go for punk. I had rainbow dreadlocks and safety pins in my ears. I embodied a surfer girl aesthetic for a year even though I'd never stood on a surfboard. In college I mainly wore my boyfriend's clothes. I liked how baggy his T-shirts were. Sometimes I'd wear his large old man's boxer shorts underneath a dress. I liked how unsexy they made me feel, but safe at the same time. Femininity with a secret layer of manliness.

When these unwanted changes made me feel out of control I sought comfort in food. Food was my friend, enemy, and refuge. I began bingeing on bags of Doritos, pastries, and loaves of bread while telling my body: "Fuck you, I control you, I can do what I want." But the full, sickly feeling didn't feel like rebellion, it made me feel even more gross and horrible. I began purging after a binge. I bought laxatives. I made my stomach feel sick from chugging liters of water after I ate an entire cake.

Sometimes I'd stay home from school because it was easier to avoid food that way. Then I'd freak out that I wasn't getting any exercise because going to school meant a half-hour bike ride, so instead I'd run up and down the stairs. I'd feel so hungry it felt like my insides were eating themselves, and then I'd run to the kitchen and devour whatever I could find.

I needed discipline and I needed a sense of routine, so I counted calories in everything. I'd make lists and meal plans and exercise goals and weight goals. I set arbitrary challenges for myself like:

Tuesday: eat nothing but grapes
Wednesday: only eat green food

Food was violently stripped of its simplicity and was given a new outfit: one of obsession, compulsion, and punishment.

I wasn't able to look at food differently until my early twenties. This was thanks to therapy, which helped me accept some of the things that are out of my control. However, initially I had my own tactic: don't think about food at all.

I developed this surface-level blasé attitude about what I ate: "Oh, whatever, I'm just going to drink two pints of milk and eat a loaf of bread and devour this cupcake right here—who the fuck cares?" For me, caring about what I consumed felt triggering. It would set off a fear that I'd go back to my old ways. Food would become too powerful. I'd lose myself in its hold over me. I'd be the hungry marionette with food controlling the strings. The only thing I could do was convince myself that I was beyond caring. Problem is: food is everywhere, and food triggers are everywhere.

After I worked in a theater I got my first proper London job working for a student offers and deals website. I sat at a table with women who had collectively decided to do a healthy eating challenge. What gave their plan a sinister turn for me was that they announced whoever lost the most weight by Christmas won. The winner received money they had pooled together and a pair of yoga pants.

I stopped munching on my peanut butter and sugar sandwich (FYI, when money's tight, peanut butter and sugar is the most delicious sandwich spread). I could feel a little well of anger bubble up in my stomach. I walked away from my table and did what I usually did when something frustrated me: I marched around the building. A friend caught up with me and I explained what I'd witnessed, only it came out more dramatic than I intended: "They are bad women!" I yelled. "They are bad for each other. They are being bad women. I hate them so much!"

A few years later at a different job, I had a similar episode where I actually got so mad I marched to HR after I heard a group of coworkers openly assess how many calories were in each sandwich we'd been given as a free lunch that day. It was becoming a strange ritual for that particular group. Free food would arrive and they'd stand in front of it counting calories like they were evaluating antiques at an auction. Reporting them turned me into a schoolgirl narc, but I couldn't help my reaction. On the surface I was angry, but beneath that I was frightened. I didn't want anything to send me back to teenage me, who could look at any item of food (or even a teaspoon of semen) and tell you exactly how many calories it contained.

I wish there were a way to strip away from food all the other add-ons: the shame, the control, the power. How can food ever just be food? How can you look at pizza and just see it as pizza and nothing else?

Can food ever just be food?

Something that's nudged me in the right direction was finding pride in what I'm putting into my mouth (that's what she said). I started cooking more. I'm not a great chef—in fact, the second I started showing off my slow-cooker lasagna on Instagram, I lost a ton of followers, but that's just by the by. Eating something I put together myself makes it easier for me to see it as what it is: nutrients, ingredients, sauce, a recipe, etc. The stuff I make is rarely super healthy, but it's always better than ordering pizza or falling asleep with Doritos dust on my forehead.

When looking for recipes online, the middle ground of good, hearty, healthy food is often hard to find. It tends to be either super indulgent chocolate banana pancake deep-fried in butter wrapped around a Mars bar *or* a bowl of kale with two grains of salt. It's easy to steer clear of the indulgent stuff because, frankly, I'm not that good a baker. The sad bowls of kale are harder to avoid. They're everywhere. Sad bowls of kale are an epidemic.

We've been hit by a white-lady wellness wave: there are cookbooks, Instagram accounts, YouTube series all about assembling chia bowls and milking almonds, and predominantly these come from white women with topknots and yoga pants. This is not a sweeping statement, just log on to Instagram.

A lot of the language these authors use centers around the phrase "clean eating." Clean eating basically means trying to eat as many whole foods as possible—so foods that aren't processed, refined, or handled. In short: foods that are as close to their natural form as they can be. There's nothing wrong with that if that's the kind of food that tickles your pickle (and you're making sure you're getting enough nutrients). The problem lies with the phrase "clean eating," implying that all other foods that don't meet these criteria are "dirty." Culinary queen Nigella Lawson nailed it when she was speaking on *Woman's Hour* in 2015 and said: "I think that food should not be used as a way of persecuting oneself, and I think really one should look to get pleasure about what's good rather than think either, 'Oh no, that's dirty, bad, or sinful,' or, 'eating is virtuous.'"

Nigella became my food idol for many reasons. Her cooking shows are dazzlingly pornographic. For starters, she's the most beautiful being who has ever graced this planet, which makes watching her an incredibly sexy experience. But there's also something so joyful in the way in which she prepares her food and how she eats it when she's done. I particularly remember a shot of her in silk pajamas going down to her fridge at midnight to eat one of her leftover cheese soufflés. There was no shame or secrecy, the woman just fancied a fucking soufflé. It's hers. She can have it. No big deal.

Nigella taught me to love cooking for other people. To share what I've made and bask in the glow of compliments about my food (even if my pie is undercooked and people are pretty much chomping on raw dough). She taught me how to relax when I make food and how it can be meditative. Stirring risotto for an hour while playing Whitney Houston's greatest hits in the background is one of the most wonderful experiences in the world.

I can't find this kind of joy in clean eating, or any other diets for that matter. When I purchased a few of the apps that belong to some of these clean-eating ambassadors, it struck me how restrictive they were, and not to mention expensive. I was running to Whole Foods on my lunch break to get spices and powder and shakes of things I still can't pronounce. I wanted to be as happy as the girl doing a headstand, drinking my home-brewed kombucha, but my depression, lack of money, stress, and inability to even do a headstand were all getting in the way. I was blaming myself for not being able to attain the lifestyle I was seeing prescribed to me. I couldn't keep up.

Food fads are rife, and the science around food is incredibly conflicting. One day a headline will tell you blueberries might cure your bipolar, but the next day blueberries give you terrible acne. Reading these headlines and studies, I found myself yet again feeling like I couldn't keep up. So I stopped. I stopped trying to impose rules other people have created (often without proper research) on my own life. Articles where a blond lady in yoga pants tells me gluten is toxic will go straight into the trash. As will a podcast I listened to not that long ago about hormones in food driving women clinically insane. After listening I got so paranoid I started tearing down my shower curtain (apparently there are hormones in shower curtains— WHO KNEW?). Thank god I have my trusty friend Kelly, a science editor at BuzzFeed, who will tell me that it's safe to keep my shower curtains up, gluten won't kill me, and blueberries won't make my mental health any worse.

Striking up a good relationship with food has been hard work. What you eat and how it makes you feel can be such a minefield, and figuring it all out is still very much a work in progress, but here are some things I learned along the way:

- I try to pay attention to what I'm eating and limit the times I eat mindlessly while watching repeats of *The Office* on my laptop. I pay close attention to the taste and texture of

what I'm chewing on, and even when I'm hungry as hell I try not to wolf anything down.

- I've started to tell myself I actually deserve good food. I deserve to feel healthy. I deserve to roast vegetables and eat spicy peaches and smashed avocado. I deserve to spend money on fresh ingredients. I deserve to wake up feeling like I can handle the day instead of being weighed down by what I ate the night before.

- Greengrocers are a godsend. I sadly moved away from the best greengrocer in London on Newington Green, but I used to cram my basket full of fresh ingredients and walk out having only spent a fiver. It changed how I thought about food and what I considered to be a good meal. I now wanted at least three different kinds of veg with everything I was making. I wanted to use spices and sea salt and coconut oil. When you only pop down to your corner shop or your Tesco Express, you forget that you can walk a little farther and probably find vegetables and fruit that are fresher and cheaper.

- Don't compare what's on your plate to what's on someone else's. Just because your friend is eating a salad doesn't mean you have to as well. Similarly, if everyone else is tucking into steak and spare ribs, but you really fancy something smaller, go for it.

- I try not to use food to manage my emotions, but it's a process. The more I tell myself not to stress eat, the more I end up doing it. So I have tried to change the foods I do still stress eat—instead of eating raw cake batter I'll try almonds or apricots or rice cakes covered in chocolate.

- I try not to buy my drug foods. There are certain foods that when I have them in my house I eat them in one go. I have to. They're too dangerous for me; even talking about them makes me drool. French Fancies snack cakes will be consumed within ten minutes, and not just one, nope, it'll be the whole box. Same with ketchup-flavored chips, jars of peanut butter, and apple pie. I once threw away half an apple pie so I wouldn't eat the entire thing, only to dig it out of the trash and eat it with my hands. Classy.

My body and I have been on a long journey together. I'm trying to recognize it as a place I live in. A place that gives me a home. I spent years draping towels and sheets over mirrors in my house so I wouldn't have to be confronted with the monstrosity I considered my body to be. I don't do that anymore. I try and look at myself properly at least once a week. Full-frontal nudity, straight into the mirror. I try to say a couple of things about what I'm seeing. It can't be anything negative, but it doesn't have to be overtly positive either. I usually start with: "I have a mole on my butt," "My right nipple goes into hiding," or, "My lower belly sticks out." On a good day I might add, "and that's pretty cute."

HOW TO BE NICE TO YOUR BODY

One word: dance. Dance for so long you literally forget what it's like to feel self-conscious. Dance in the dark, in your chair, dance while lying in bed. Close your eyes and move your body the way you feel like. No one's watching, do whatever weird movement comes into your head.

Have a really fucking luxurious bath. Put Drake on in the background. Add rose petals to the water. Get as many bubbles as you can handle. Touch your body, all over. You don't have to feel anything, you don't have to shout, *"I love my lady lumps"* from the rooftops. Just acknowledge that you have a body, that it's yours, and that you're grateful for it.

Your body isn't made of problem zones. There are no bad patches or gross bits. See your body as a whole.

Your body isn't made of problem zones.

It's not a cage, it's a canvas. It's not a prison, it's a spaceship that will take you wherever you want to go.

Decorate your body the way you want to. I like tattoos and cheap supermarket hair dye. Maybe you want a nipple piercing or a shaved head, or maybe bangs are radical enough for you.

Don't respond to people who don't treat your body with respect. Don't respond to people who misgender you. Don't respond to people who ignore you.

Treat your body like a garden; you need water to grow your hair, you need sunlight and attention. You need nourishing. You can't punish a garden and expect it to grow. You can't chop it up, tear pieces out, slice off branches, and expect it to bloom.

Appreciate all the things your body can do and don't berate it for the things it can't.

Fill your social feeds, your scrapbook, your saved images with people you admire. People who look similar to you and people who say fuck you to beauty standards and hold themselves defiantly.

Remember that women are often made to feel like their body is an enemy. That men use our bodies, transfer their desires onto our skin, and give us no choice but to go with it. When I was growing up, I blamed my big ass for street harassment and catcalling. I blamed my breasts for all the times teachers looked down my top and made me feel uncomfortable. I blamed my long legs for when my skirt rode up and someone sitting down on the train tried to peer up it. My body made me feel disgusting; it was a magnet for unwanted attention. But my body never deserved that loathing—other people who are unable to respect the female body are the ones to blame.

Remember that your body is a miracle machine: your skin replaces itself once a month, you have 62,000 miles' worth of veins, and you create 180 million red blood cells every hour. In short: your body is a badass. It deserves your respect and admiration.

Hug yourself, fondle your breasts, stroke your pubes. Say "you're the best" or "you rock," or whatever it is you'd like someone to say to you, say it to your body.

CHAPTER 6

Remember This When You're Falling in Love

Now that you've assembled even just a small amount of self-love, you're in the right shape to get out there and date your socks off. Dating is always nerve-racking, but dating with anxiety feels like you're taking a wailing baby with you wherever you go. Yes, this restaurant is nice, but there's a screaming toddler on my lap. How am I supposed to give off a good impression when I'm trying to keep a tidal wave of panic from rising out of my stomach? I want to come across Michelle Pfeiffer-esque (specifically Pfeiffer circa *Grease 2*), but

I feel a lot more like that girl from *The Exorcist*. Messy, possessed, and devilishly horny.

To me, dating has always felt like a job interview or the first week at a new job. You're trying to figure out if you're a good fit. You have to be your best, most interesting, impressive self while trying to find out as much about the other person as possible. I give myself credit for being quite good at asking questions. I'm inquisitive and genuinely find most people interesting, but I have to make sure I don't veer into full on interrogating them.

When the questions get flipped the other way around and I'm on the receiving end, I struggle. I freeze and try to scrape the barrel of my brain for an interesting fact about myself but I come up empty. I want to tell the person about how my shoulders are double-jointed, but instead I mumble

something like, "Shuh du juh," which is met by even more panic, so I compensate by barfing up an endless stream of random and often inappropriate facts about myself, from what I ate that day, what my cup size is, and that sometimes my OCD is so bad I have to repeat everything you say under my breath three times.

For all the anxiety dating has caused me, I've never sworn off dating completely. Whenever I've been single, I've thrown myself into a flurry of dates to keep trying out new strategies until some sort of action plan sticks. I've carried with me a repertoire of stories I considered to be interesting so my brain freeze wouldn't be so detrimental.

My go-to I'm-on-a-date-and-there's-silence story has always been this random fact about Singapore airport. I actually have no idea if this is true or not, but apparently if your flight is delayed for more than five hours you get a free tour of the city *and* you get to use their pool for free. (If you work at Singapore airport and you know this is in fact a lie, can you please inform the dozens of guys in London who I've told this to?) I'd use this story, or any of my probably false airport facts, as a starting point to ease my nerves (did you know that in 1987, American Airlines saved $40,000 by removing one olive from each salad served in first class?).

The only problem is I relied so much on my airport facts that I'd start to lose track of who I'd used them on and who I hadn't. On date two I'd whip out my fact about Sydney to Dallas being the longest flight in distance and realize I'd already used that one on the first date, or maybe even just an hour earlier. Slowly, my handy tool became my worst enemy. I sounded like a glitchy Furby spewing out airport facts until I ran out of batteries.

So how did I learn to chill out? In short: I didn't. The biggest thing I learned is that I'm always going to be stressed. There will be dates where I'm not *as* stressed, and this has a lot to do with the person I'm with. It's the little things people do that make anxious daters feel at ease. For some reason, when my date actually uses my name (e.g., "Nice to meet you, Maggy," or, "Maggy, where did you grow up?"), it feels like they think I'm important and worthy of their time. When someone is friendly to the waiter I feel like they're polite and I can trust them. When they're all right drinking but not constantly rushing to the bar to get another round I feel like we can have a good time without getting wrecked.

There are a few things I can do myself to feel more comfortable. First, recruit help from elsewhere. When I'm walking to wherever I'm meeting my date, I like to be on the phone with a friend. Someone who won't mind that I suddenly hang up when I spot my date, and someone who won't mind my running commentary as I'm looking for the venue: *"OMG, I can see them. Should I wave? No. No I won't wave. I'll be OK. Gotta go they've spotted me bye!"*

Once I'm on my date I need to have quick access to water.

> So how did I learn to chill out? In short: I didn't.

Water eases my anxiety. Without water I panic that I might get dehydrated and shrivel like a prune on the spot. I also get paranoid about choking on food on a date. When my whole body is riddled with nerves the simple act of swallowing a bit of veggie burger demands all my attention. I need water to help move things down.

I always carry water with me wherever I go. Whether it's a date, a job interview, a train journey, or a bike ride. Water is so unequivocally good for you, you know the second it hits your body you're doing a good thing.

Dating also involves not dating. The bits in between where you're worrying, stressing out, figuring how and when to respond. If things have gone well and a second date is in the cards, I hover around my phone like a thirsty animal hangs around a spring. It's a life source. If I get a text from my date I'll feel instantly better, energized, and happy about the world. If the well's run dry and he's a no-show, I feel miserable and rejected.

After being ghosted millions of times, I've succumbed to the school of "He's Just Not That Into You," a phrase made famous by the self-help book from the early 2000s of the same title and a subsequent film. I repeated that phrase over and over throughout my dating life. It was helpful in that it allowed me to shrug off deadbeat guys instantly, but it was unhelpful in that I said it too often and too quickly. Even if a guy took an hour instead of ten minutes to reply, I'd say that out loud like a mantra. I'd be breaking up with the guy before we even started dating.

When my current boyfriend, Alex, and I were arranging one of our earlier dates, there was a point when it had been a week and a bit since we'd last seen each other. I was in the height of my "Yep, pretty sure this guy doesn't like me" phase. He'd not read some of my WhatsApp messages while he had been online, so I'd assumed he was off boning the rest of London and had forgotten to keep me informed. He was too hot for me anyway. It just wasn't going to happen.

To my surprise he got in touch on a Friday night after he'd come back from a work trip to ask how my night was going. At that time I was in the back of an Uber going home from the pub. Alex and I sent a few back-and-forth texts about our respective evenings, and somewhere in the middle of the conversation we apparently arranged to meet up the next day. I went to bed feeling happy and excited.

When I woke up it was as if my memory had been wiped. Our conversation had been swallowed up in the black hole of my "everything is awful" thinking. Because I'd spent a few weeks stewing in this feeling of "oh he definitely didn't like me," I'd gotten too used to it, like a hoodie that smells and makes you look a bit square-shaped but you wear it anyway because you've had it for ages and it's sort of comfortable.

A friend of mine called me in the morning and asked what I was doing with my day, and I moaned about how this guy I really liked wasn't really reciprocating and I thought we'd have another date by now, but it's just not going to happen, woe is me etc., etc., etc. She told me to go back to bed. Wait a few hours. Text him, and if he didn't get back I'd go to her house and we'd do something fun.

We hung up. I put *Seinfeld* on and grabbed a bag of Doritos. This was going to be my Saturday now. At 1 p.m. I got a text from Alex: "Hey, running five minutes late. See you soon!"

Soon?

Sooon?

SOOOOOON?

My heart crashed into the pit of my stomach. Where was he going? What did he mean he was running late? Where were we meeting? Why didn't I realize we'd made a plan? I raced through our text message exchange and it hit me: 1 p.m. Somerset House. It was right there. Flashing at me. Fuck fuck fuck fuck fuck.

At the time, my flat was ninety minutes away from Somerset House by train, and I'd used my monthly "fuck it, just get an Uber" allowance the night before. I texted a thousand apologies to Alex hoping desperately he wouldn't be offended by my lateness. Because he's an actual nice normal person he said not to worry. He was going to do some shopping and he'd wait for me in the café.

Imagine if my brain wasn't wired to automatically assume the worst in a situation. Instead of rushing I could have had a wonderful, relaxing Saturday morning, with plenty of time to get ready and feel confident. Instead, I had to sprint through London with sweat cascading down my armpits.

YOU DON'T HAVE TO TELL ANYONE ABOUT YOUR MENTAL HEALTH

If your mental health condition affects your day-to-day life, you might feel inclined to share what you're going through with whomever you're dating. When, where, and how you do this is entirely up to you. It's your information. You own it. No one can force you to give anything away you don't want to.

When I was at a friend's party at a pub for her thirty-eighth birthday, I was stuck talking to an Irish pastry chef. I say stuck because the pub is shaped like a narrow corridor. Once you're standing next to someone, that's kind of your spot for the rest of the night. So from the get go: not a great location for someone with anxiety.

Pastry Chef was bald, with deep-sea blue eyes and a tribal tattoo around his bicep. He asked me what I did for a living. I told him that I write.

"What kind of stuff do you write?"

"Mainly pieces on mental health."

"Oh. *Oh*."

He took a step back like I'd just spat out a dirty word and a warning sign flared between us. This wasn't a guy I was going to get along with. He then went on to make it even worse: "Oh I know some real mental girls. Like *really* mental."

First: this man was in his forties, aka a grown-ass man. He should know better than to refer to women as girls, unless he's literally talking about a child, which he wasn't. Then there's the fact that in his statement he drew that dividing line between him (a sane person) and all these women he supposedly knows (the crazies), implying that they were in the wrong and he was a victim.

Pastry Chef detected a slight eye roll in my expression and began to excuse his statement by telling me all about his ex who had bipolar and how she ruined his life. "She should have told me she was bipolar. I should have been prepared." I didn't know what to say to that. I had only just met him. I felt like I didn't want him to unload his and his ex's history on me. He decided to change gears: "Do you write from experience then?" I nodded. "What's wrong with you?" He said this in a jokey way, making his blue eyes glow, but I was not going to fall for it that easily.

"Nothing's wrong with me. I have borderline personality disorder with a side of depression and anxiety." I then did an over-the-top curtsy and looked around for an escape route, but he still wasn't quite done.

"Do you tell people you date you have mental problems?"

"Eventually, I guess."

"But the first date?"

"I don't know."

"You should tell them."

"Why?"

"Else it's false advertising."

"Huh?"

"If they don't know what's wrong with you, then it's like you're lying."

At this point the anger that had been slowly festering in my belly spread all throughout my body. I wanted to scream in this man's face, show him my full-blown crazy lady, but instead I swallowed my anger and escaped to the bathroom, where I published a series of angry tweets about the situation. I knew he wouldn't listen to me, or maybe I was too exhausted to try, and a crowded corridor shaped pub just wasn't the place to do it. I avoided him for the rest of the night, and when I got home punched my pillow a few times.

Not telling the person I'm on a first date with that I have mental health issues is not false advertising. There's more to people than whatever is going inside of their heads. Yes, sometimes that part of my life does take over and things go wobbly. Sometimes things might get so bad that relationships end or I end up hurting people, but for the most part I'm just me. I'm on a date wanting to tell you about my life, the good parts, the interesting parts, and the parts I think are more important.

When I fill someone in on my mental health issues it's always when I'm beginning to fully trust them. I know there's longevity in our relationship, it's not just a series of drunken stumblings out of pubs.

I've been incredibly fortunate that no one has reacted badly to me sharing my issues. If I can tell that the person is going to be shifty or weird about it, I probably wouldn't be attracted to them in the first place. I had a drink with someone who was talking about their ex and referring to her multiple times as a "psycho," and I thought nope, this one isn't for me. That's not the kind of guy I want to date. Maybe she wasn't great, maybe she did do some inappropriate things, but I don't know the full story. I'd hate the idea of being confined to one person's unkind description of me.

CHAPTER 7

Remember This When You're Having Sex

Sex is great. Orgasms are great. When someone kisses you so passionately you lose yourself and stars begin to waltz around your head and everything is dreamy and lovely, that too is great. However, it's not always like this.

I've launched myself into sex so quickly there's not a lot of passion involved. It's hard, fast, painful, and destructive. I've used my body like a sex doll, hoping someone can bring it to life again. Sex won't bring it to life—self-care and self-respect and genuinely being OK will bring it to life. Having someone thrust their fingers inside me so deep it hurts isn't me enjoying myself or having a great time. I'm self-harming, and I'm using someone else to do it.

Having borderline personality disorder (BPD) makes the casual sex difficult too. I feel things very intensely very quickly, and the guy I met at a house party who I fuck but have zero things in common with can quickly become the absolute best man in the world and OMG I cannot wait for our children to pop out of my vagina. Even without BPD, I'm a hopeless romantic. I like the idea of meet cutes and love at first sight. I want an instant connection, but I want it so much that I force it at times.

In my worst moments I've resorted to sex in the futile hope to feel something again. I'd fuck people I knew were bad for me, but in my head I dressed them up as saviors. I'd give my entire body to them and define myself in their gaze. I'd be a sucker for bullshit compliments and pickup lines. I've met up with guys who had girlfriends and I didn't care. I've met guys who'd say things like, "I don't normally do this," and not cared that this was probably a fabricated line they told everyone. I got them to come home with me, and told myself that surely this means there's something good about me.

I became hooked on having sex with people in this meaningless, vapid way, all the while hoping secretly it would lead to something more. I'd sleep with an ex and fuckboys I didn't know, and flirt with sleazy divorced men. In my mind it was possible something could happen out of these encounters, but once the spell was over I'd go home cursing myself for being the way I am. That married man I made out with on the District line is definitely not going to be the one to save me from myself. Especially not with his hand up my skirt or his tongue down my throat.

This period of my life felt a lot like I was running around London, glass of wine in hand, trying to find myself. I look at the clothes I bought in this time, all tight black dresses; booby and high-heeled. There's nothing wrong with donning your tightest dress and hitting the town when you feel like it, but I was doing this every night. I was defining myself by how much I could get people to want to have sex with me. I wanted so much to feel safe and secure, but instead sabotaged my safety by making bad decisions.

I still haven't quite figured out how to differentiate good sex and bad sex. You're not always going to have sex with someone you love, so that can't be the defining factor. I think a lot of it has to do with trusting your gut. The feeling deep down in your belly that knows what's wrong and what's right—or at the very least what feels safe. I've ditched perfectly lovely evenings with friends because some guy I didn't care about texted me and wanted me to meet up with him. In my head I felt like that would be more beneficial for me, that I'd get something out of it. In hindsight, having a quiet night with friends, talking, making jokes would have been so much better.

I'm learning how to make better decisions for myself, and how to protect myself in doing so. I'm trying to give a voice to that feeling that says "this isn't OK" and act on it when I hear it. I'm lucky in that I have a boyfriend now who I have a brilliant and very sexual relationship with. If I say no it's an immediate no, there's no pressure, and at no point do I feel obliged to do something I don't have to do. I feel like this might be very "Yeah, duh! That should be the norm!" to a lot of people. And it should, but when your sense of self has been obliterated by depression and self-destruction, it's not always easy to demand the things you know are right for you. It's a learning process, and one I feel like I'm finally getting the hang of.

CHAPTER 8

Remember This When You're in a Relationship

Well done! You've survived the mind fuck that's dating and you're in a proper hold-hands-when-you're-walking-down-the-street kind of relationship. Unless you're like me and holding hands makes you recoil. Then maybe you link pinkies or touch each other's fingertips every now and again. Either way, you're in it. You've found someone you love spending time with. You hang out often. You have sex. Your friends think they're great, and then the inevitable happens. That great period in the beginning of every relationship, where everything is fun and easy, becomes less bright. Like an old T-shirt that loses its color in the wash, things feel a little less sparkly between the two of you (bear with it though because old T-shirts are always my fave and get worn the most).

You might start bickering more, you cry in front of each other for the first time, and some of your behaviors that you hated about yourself in past relationships crawl back in, whether it's paranoia, insecurity, jealousy, being a nitpicker, etc.

Part of it is inevitable, because if two people spend a lot of time together they get to know each other. Not the surface-level stuff, but the stuff underneath it all, the stuff that troubles and scares you, and it can't all be pretty.

It's this part of a relationship I find super hard to navigate because I'm such an *all-or-nothing* person. If I'm arguing with someone, even if it's just a little quibble, in my head we are shouting at each other and we might as well just break up because this is so awful see you later bye! I'm so quick to write things off, and it's not because I want to, it's because deep down there's a distinct feeling that I don't deserve to be loved. It sounds super dramatic and emo, but if there's a thing about me that someone wanting to be my partner should know it's that. It's where all my weird behaviors come from. I genuinely feel that there's something so inherently off about me that anyone who says they love me must be full of absolute shit, or worse: I've tricked them.

I try my very best to fight against this feeling, and the more I'm honest about it with the person I'm with, the better. I might freak out about something really mundane, and it's not because I'm overly insecure or jealous—I don't actually think they're about to run off with that hot girl they keep liking on Instagram. It's because my brain is gathering evidence to support my hypothesis: no one can love me. Some relationships make it easier to gather this kind of evidence. I have been with people who have cheated on me, or not cheated but pretty much cheated. On the flipside I've been in relationships that actually have been good, and yet I spin them around to fit my theory that they don't truly love me.

It's how I blew through a series of relationships over the past couple of years. Repeating the pattern of dating someone, falling in love, having them say they love me, and then working my way to make them fall out of love because I never really believed them in the first place.

Love to me seems like a bar of soap that keeps slipping out of my hands. Each time I think I know what it is, its definition changes completely. Every time I think I'm in love I feel like this is nothing like it was before, this time it's love, like love-love, and that thing a year ago must have been something else.

Changing my relationship ways hasn't been the easiest thing in the world. I do sometimes run down the street crying over a problem I've created in my head, but I'm also learning that that isn't solely my fault. Feeling deeply unlovable is lonely, and it's shitty, and it's tiring. I didn't wake up and choose to feel like that. I don't carry that feeling around with me on purpose because it's fun or interesting. It's carrying a bunch of dead weight for no reason. It's in my way, it gets in other people's way. I hate it.

Thanks to therapy and having a boyfriend I really, really want to make all the effort in the world for, I'm learning to forgive myself for past relationship fuck-ups. I'm learning to stop thinking of myself as the worst/ugliest/smelliest/dumbest person ever. I'm learning that I have something good to add to a relationship. I'm a good partner. I care about people. I can make people happy. It's not a big magic trick; it's real and it's possible.

> I'm learning to stop thinking of myself as the worst/ugliest/smelliest/dumbest person ever.

I've also tried to devise a little checklist for when my brain is ready to jump to conclusions. (Caveat: sometimes jumping to conclusions is the right thing to do, like when I spotted a guy I was dating religiously liking everything a female colleague of ours was doing on Instagram, and *Bam!* after he dumped me they ended up together. However, generally, that isn't how it works.) When I can feel a little spark in the pit of my stomach making me feel like unwanted drama is on the horizon, I try my hardest to pause for just one little second and go through this handy list:

- Stop what you're thinking about before the spiral of thoughts continues. Just stop for a second and examine those thoughts—what's going on? What's worrying you? What are you afraid of?

■ Voice some of the thoughts out loud. I'm luckily dating someone now who is the most patient man in the world, so he's OK with me asking him a million questions a day. This is how a typical conversation will go:

Me: Do you love me?
Him: Yes
Me: But do you like me?
Him: Yeah, of course
Me: But do you like me as an actual person?
Him: Yes
Me: OK. Pizza?

■ Don't lump all the people you've ever dated in one big ball. Sometimes patterns develop in a relationship that you might recognize from a relationship before, and if they're valid warning signs—like they make you feel bad about yourself—then you need to absolutely listen to those. But if they're just little everyday things, don't think: "Oh, my ex used to tell me off for leaving my clothes all over the floor, here we go again, another guy trying to change me, oh my god all men are terrible." Now I just say: "Look, I'm a messy person, I'll tidy when I feel like it, there's no point trying to get me to change." That way the progression of the relationship can go in its own direction rather than just follow the course of my past ones where tiny fights about me being messy escalate tenfold.

CHAPTER 9

Remember This When Someone Else Hurts You

Relationships, the good ones at least, are about letting people disarm your steely wall of self-protection because you feel comfortable and safe. You're getting to know each other and you feel comfortable showing them other parts of your life they haven't seen before.

To get to this point, you need a good understanding of what your own boundaries are, because you can't always choose who enters your life and in what shape they'll exit. People who are good to you will listen to your cues and leave when you want them to, but they'll stay put when you need help. In short: they respect your boundaries.

As a very simplified definition, boundaries tend to be physical or psychological. Your physical boundary is pretty self-explanatory: the barrier between you and someone or something else. Psychological boundaries are complex. In the essay "The Unthinkable Boundaries of Self," Professor Ciarán Benson writes that psychological boundaries are tied up with acts of possessing or of owning. They include what belongs to you (things, people, ideas, skills, rights, reputations, privileges, etc.). Essentially, things you control and call your own. They also encompass the way in which you belong to others (forms of solidarity, group identity, obligation, etc.) that control and have claim on you. In this sense, what people own, and how they are themselves owned, helps make them the sort of people they are.

When you're sensitive or anxious or you've experienced trauma in your life, you might have a complicated relationship with your psychological boundaries. There's a push-pull in terms of what you feel you have ownership over, and how others have ownership over you.

I have steely walls I set up to protect myself from the outside world. It's such a mess in my head that my boundaries are largely there for self-preservation. I need room to reinstate some kind of equilibrium. If people come too close, they could throw me off my game even more. However, sometimes I push too hard and I'm left in a lonely room in my brain with an aching longing for companionship, but it's too late to let someone in.

When someone oversteps my boundaries by doing something I'm not comfortable with I retreat even further into myself. I shut down. The space I choose to take up in this world becomes smaller, I become smaller; my hopes and demands and my voice all shrink at once.

It's in these moments I try to recall someone who I think had the right idea. Someone who defended her boundaries like a proud landowner shooing away poachers.

I was accompanying Antonia, a classmate, on a shopping trip to the mall. She was my age, fourteen, at the time. Her hair was dusty blond, she had a belly button ring and wore neon laces in her Converse. She had a spark, and whenever I saw her she seemed to possess a confidence most teenage girls lacked. Her hair was always ironed straight and she flicked it often like she was flinging a handbag over her shoulder. Although I was considerably taller than her, my long, lanky legs struggled to keep up with her quick stride.

We were walking through the food court to reach the escalators at the end of the mall. She wanted to get some new hoop earrings. I wanted to get whatever she was getting. Anything that could bring me closer to being a little bit more like her.

A large group of older boys passed us and I clenched my fists knowing what was about to come. At the very least, they'd make some kind of remark; at the worst they'd try to touch us. This shopping mall had become a hot spot for sexual harassment. Boys at least five years older than me would touch my arm, my butt, or follow me around as I tried to find the exit. I still went back though. My lust for Dunkin' Donuts surpassed the stress of having my body poked and prodded. I had learned to always wear long skirts in the mall. I'd brush my long bangs over my face and tie my sweater around my waist to hide any curves.

Despite my armor of layers, I knew we'd be no match for this large group of pulsating testosterone. The guys passed us, and to no one's surprise sucked their tongues and said something I couldn't hear, but it was bound to be rude. I closed my eyes and increased my pace, hoping Antonia would do the same. She did the opposite. The boys slowed down and she stopped right in front of them. She stared the leader of the pack straight in the eyes: *"No!"* she shouted at him. Her voice wasn't shrill or scared, it was firm and strong and delightfully terrifying. *"Don't do that again."* She took my hand and we marched farther along the mall, down the escalators, and straight to Claire's Accessories. I wanted to hug her, but she was too busy looking for earrings. Antonia hadn't done anything out of the ordinary for her. She'd recognized an uncomfortable situation and stood up for herself. She used her voice to reaffirm her boundary. She told anyone who wanted to fuck with her that they couldn't overstep the line. She wouldn't let them.

I wanted with every fiber in my being to soak up some of Antonia's badassery, but never quite got there. My "no" was never loud like Antonia's, but more a meek whisper. I didn't know how to sound like her.

I never found out how to unleash my inner Antonia—in fact my boundaries became more inflexible as I grew older. They are watertight. I don't like being touched. I don't like it when people sit too close to me. There's a force field around me.

Through doing that arduous task of growing up, I realized how boundaries can be tied up to your emotional space, which often manifests itself in what you choose to reveal to people. When I'm nervous I have no problem making fun of myself, often sharing an inappropriate story to do with sex or farting or falling over. It's a way to laugh at myself before anyone else can.

If all this talk about boundaries has you confused here's a list of some of the times I felt people disrespected my boundaries in small, sometimes even barely noticeable ways, so you can see what I mean:

- When someone (usually a man) yells, "Oi, darling, give us a smile!" I don't have a choice whether or not I want to hear his order because he's right in my ear
- When I'm sitting with someone who finds it funny that I hate being physically close to people so they move their chair right in front of me
- When I was fourteen and some boys at school cornered me in the locker room asking if I'd ever fingered myself

- When someone I didn't know very well sent me a photo of their penis without me asking
- When I'm meeting up with an old boyfriend and we're having a nice talk, but out of the blue he leans in for a kiss and I almost tumble off my chair to avoid having his mouth land on my face
- When a man on the Tube decides to stand even closer to me so he can look down my top
- When someone repeatedly asks me questions about my sex life when the conversation isn't about sex at all
- When someone tells me a massive secret that I didn't ask for
- When I'm in a group and someone decides to tell my story to the group as if it's theirs
- When I'm tickled
- When I get pulled onto someone's lap
- When someone shakes my hand and puts their other hand onto our handshake making it like a hand prison
- When someone shows up at my house after I've told them I want space
- When someone acts like they're my therapist and tries to diagnose me
- When someone assumes something about me without checking first
- When someone reads my diaries
- When someone goes through my in-box
- When someone gives me unsolicited advice
- When someone tells me they think I should go off my meds

THE REALLY, REALLY BAD THING
THAT HAPPENED

What I'm about to tell you was the most difficult part of writing this book. I wrote it all down because it was a reminder to myself that despite the cage of boundaries I set up, self-protection can be limited. Sometimes people break through, they force their way in, and they hurt you more than you ever thought was possible.

Trigger warning: I'm about to describe what happened in all its unfortunate detail.

Nearly half a million adults are sexually assaulted in England and Wales each year. After it happened to me, I felt unsafe, I felt ashamed, and I felt like it was my fault. Slowly I patched myself up, but not completely, because the thread still unravels sometimes, but I did eventually learn to trust people again.

The night of my assault was doomed from the start. I was twenty-six. Post breakup, post trying to set my arm on fire outside the pub, I had plasters on my skin, but my life still had many cracks in it. I needed change desperately, and while I was being proactive, I'd had one of those days that seemed to be an assembly line of bad news.

I'd had two job interviews, and both seemed extremely promising. However, both interviewers called me one after the other that day to tell me I hadn't made the cut; they liked me, but someone else was better suited. I slumped into my therapist's chair at 5 p.m. completely deflated. She had some news of her own: she was pregnant. The pregnancy was likely going to be quite rough due to several complications and she needed to stop working. I leaped up and congratulated her, but she gently nudged me to sit back down again.

"Do you understand what this means for our sessions?"

I did a slow nod, which she rightly interpreted as a no. I didn't realize this would be the end of the road for us. I'd have to choose a new therapist and I'd have to start again with someone else. Deep down I also felt a sense of rejection, like she was choosing her baby over me. I should have used this opportunity to voice these concerns, but instead I just shrugged and said I was so happy for her.

I ignored the thunderbolt of panic that struck my chest. I ignored the worry; the fear that I'd have nowhere else to go. I'd come to depend on these weekly sessions. I'd store up all the worries whizzing around my head and pour them out slowly drop by drop whenever we met. I liked her a lot. She was kind and warm and foreign in London like me, but she was leaving me. In a few weeks I'd never see her again.

Once I was out of my session I smoked a few cigarettes and walked to the National Portrait Gallery, where I was meeting an old friend I hadn't seen in years. We'd spotted that we both lived in London on Facebook and decided to meet up for a drink. At this point I was caught up in a lot of dating drama and thought it would be a relief to spend an evening with an old friend. It would be safe and pleasant and fun, like meeting up with a cousin.

On my way to the museum I thought I saw my ex-boyfriend on the street. My heart started pounding, and I panicked, worried about how to act casual. It turned out not to be him. I felt relieved and stupid all at once. All that adrenaline for nothing.

My friend arrived and we hugged, and I told him my lame story about not bumping into my ex. He guided us to a pub. I was so desperate for a drink it was like I'd been out in the desert and I'd finally spotted a water tank. I hadn't realized my friend had booked a fancy restaurant in Soho for after the pub. I thought this night would just be a couple of drinks and then that's it. I ordered another large glass of wine and thought "Fuck it." I'd had a shit day, I knew he was kind of loaded and would probably pay for the dinner, and I wanted to make the most of this.

At the restaurant I drank more. I wasn't engaged in our conversation. I was thinking about my job situation, my ex and me, all the wine I was still planning on drinking. There were times in my conversation with my friend that felt a bit off. He touched my wrist at one point. Gently nudged my knee with his hand. Stared at my face for a second too long which made me think, "Wait, this isn't just friendly anymore." I was getting drunker and my feelings of discomfort were pushed aside by intoxication.

After dinner I wanted to go home, but he suggested we go for one more drink. In the pub I drank more, and then in another pub where I drank more still. From this point on my memory stops. Thinking back to it is like staring into a bucket of black paint. There's nothing there. I can't see a thing.

When I regained consciousness I could feel that I was in a bed. I was horizontal. There were sheets beneath me. The ceiling was white, the window was open, and it was morning. There was a sharp pain in my lower body. I opened my eyes. My friend's naked body was thrusting in and out of me. I closed my eyes again. Last night's alcohol twinged my stomach. This wasn't happening. I couldn't have this happen to me. I needed to say no, I needed to make a sound, but I couldn't, I couldn't open my mouth. I squeezed my eyes shut and escaped back into my head. I thought if I could just drift outside of my body maybe my body could disappear too.

When I found myself fully disconnected from the lifeless blob of flesh below me I found I wasn't the only person hovering over my body, I had company. There was my ex I thought I'd seen the day before and his mum and his dad and his sister and her husband. They were all people I knew I'd hurt when I broke up with my ex. I imagined them standing there cheering the act on, telling me I deserved this. They were a Greek chorus of hate. I knew none of these people would ever want this to happen to me, but in my hallucination it felt extremely real. It felt like what was happening to my body below was justified.

When the man I thought was my friend finally stopped, he lay down and trapped me in a sweaty hug. I reinhabited my body. I felt the hair on his chest. I could smell his sweat, his morning breath. I hated it. I hated everything, but I still felt unable to move. My mind and body hadn't fully connected yet.

I slid out of his embrace and went to his bathroom, where I dry-heaved into the toilet. I couldn't throw up. I wanted to purge the terrible evening, but I wasn't able to. He asked if I was OK and I said I was going to go home. I put my clothes on and switched on the autopilot part of my brain. I had to get home. I had to get through this.

I remember being walked to the bus stop. I remember trying hard to be friendly. I remember he hugged me good-bye and I could feel the vomit rise again. I remember getting on the bus only to get off again. I remember a McDonald's loo. I remember staring at some gum stuck on a wall. I remember getting back on the bus. I remember getting home, taking my clothes off, and wrapping myself up in a duvet.

I remember feeling like something awful had happened, but I wasn't quite sure what.

WHAT TO DO AFTER

After that night it felt like someone had knocked all the insides out of my body. If you tapped my skull you could hear the echo reverberate to my toes: I was empty. The parts of my brain controlling everyday things like appetite and tiredness had tangled together into a knot. I didn't know what was going on, what I was doing, or what I was feeling.

I told the story of that night to myself over and over and even branched out to a few close friends. I hoped that by imposing a narrative on that blurred evening I could turn it into something that made sense, something I could manage. But every time I divulged a bit of information, or made the story more real, it became harder for me to believe. Did this really happen? Am I *sure* it's not my fault? I was the one drinking. Did I do this?

I wish there had been some kind of guide, or a quiz, to help marshal the flurry of worries that consumed me. Did you black out? Yes. Go straight to question three. Did it hurt? Yes. Go to your GP now. Was it unprotected? Yes. Go to the sexual health clinic.

It took me awhile and a lot of stumbling through a flurry of mixed-up thought processes to finally come to terms with the fact that I didn't give consent. It was sexual assault. I was unconscious. That man had sex with me against my will.

Everyone's experience of sexual violence is different, so unfortunately there can't be a blueprint for what to do after it's happened, but here are some things I learned that might be helpful if you've been through this too.

1. Whatever You're Doing, It's OK

There is no one-size-fits-all reaction. Whether you find your-self climbing the walls, shouting in your pillow, swearing at people who are trying to support you—these are acceptable reactions. A lot of my responses trickled in a lot later and I found myself lashing out at people who were helping me. I was dating someone who was patient with me, and yet after we'd have sex I'd cry and call him terrible names, as if all my anger was directed at him, not the attacker.

I felt extremely guilty for my behavior during this time but after speaking to psychologist Dr. Nina Burrowes, I realized that whatever I had to do, I simply had to do it. You have to give yourself permission to go through the inevitable emotional roller coaster. The more you stifle yourself, the bumpier that roller coaster can get. Dr. Bur-rowes also shared with me an incredible piece of advice that kept coming back to me: have compassion for yourself. Whatever you're doing, it's your way of dealing with it. You've got to give yourself some slack.

> Have compassion for yourself.

2. Don't Force Yourself to Do Anything You Don't Want to Do

I was reluctant to confront the guy who did this to me, but I did feel some kind of responsibility to make sure he would never hurt anyone ever again. Perhaps this would give me some closure too? There's a lot of talk, especially on TV, about victims forgiving their attacker. Thing is, I had no desire to forgive him or to school him on his actions. My main desire was to avoid this person for the rest of my life. I didn't want to have to see him. I didn't want to talk with him.

I imagined myself walking into a café if I did arrange a meet up. I imagined how nervous I'd feel. How nauseous. How sweaty my palms would get. Just picturing my body in the same room as his body made my stomach twist. Breathing the same air. What if I could smell him? What if I dissociated on the spot? What if I retreated so far into my mind I'd never come back? What if I got drunk? What if I lost control? What if it happened again?

I lectured myself on what I believed to be my duty: my duty to confront this man was more important than my own well-being. I scolded myself for being weak and lazy. But despite my own negative self-talk, I still couldn't motivate myself to type his number into my phone. After a year of this wrestling match between what I felt I had to do and what I wanted to do, I finally deleted his number. Perhaps in a few years I'll be ready, and I'll get that number back, but right now I want to let myself live. I'm not lazy, I'm proactively putting my own mental health first. I'm letting go of invisible pressures. I'm taking it one day at a time, on my own terms.

3. Tell People When You're Ready

It's not easy starting that process of saying out loud what happened to you. You don't just have your own feelings to consider, you're thinking about the other person too: Will they believe me? How will they take this? Will they be OK?

If you want to talk to someone about what you've been through, make sure it's the right person. Just as it's vital to have compassion for yourself during this time, you have to have the headspace to have compassion for the person you're sharing your story with. It's shocking and upsetting to hear that someone you care about has been violated. If you're able to, give them space to be able to react. Try not to set them up to fail. Don't go in there with too many expectations. If you have specific needs from someone, tell them that from the outset. For example: "I would really like you to come to the police station with me," or, "I just really need someone to sit with me for a bit." That way they have a framework to work with and they'll know how to support you.

I think my biggest mistake was rushing into telling people what had happened without knowing what I wanted from them. Perhaps it would have helped if I'd said: "Look, I'm telling you this, I don't really know why, I don't know how I need you to react, so just give me some time." Instead, I blurted out my story and declared the conversation was closed, I didn't want to talk anymore. I then grew angry and resentful when that person hadn't acted the way I wanted them to, which was unfair.

If you're the person hearing this story for the first time, I'd say the most important thing is not to say anything at all—just listen. Make sure you're making your friend or relative feel safe.

4. There's No Deadline

With physical trauma you might be told that you need rest and you'll be able to walk on your sprained ankle in a week or two. Emotional healing is a slower journey. It might feel long and drawn out in parts, and other times it might feel stifling and panicky. The most important thing is to give yourself permission to breathe and to find your own pace. I'm still dealing with what happened to me, I still think about it. Scenes flash into my head when I see a blond man in a suit. I once dry-heaved into my backpack when my night bus drove past the place where it all happened.

Just when you think you've got a handle on your trauma, there's a strong possibility that your pace will change. Sometimes I'll feel like I'm sprinting toward recovery. I joined a group training session on how to watch out for signs of domestic abuse in your community. To me this felt like vindication. I felt triumphant. I was going to help someone, or at least try. But other times I feel completely consumed by fear and shame, like I've taken a million steps backward.

Often this happens arbitrarily. I was watching a TV show where a character played by Nicole Kidman gets repeatedly abused, but the situation is murky in the beginning, and there's an insinuation that part of her welcomes the abuse. During one of the episodes I felt like a spotlight had been turned on above me. I felt like I could relate to her character, even though it was such an extreme version of what I'd been through. If people at any point think Kidman's character was to blame, what about me? Surely they'd think the same. In that moment I went from eating Doritos in my bed to spinning out of control and resorting to my crutch: leaving the house and trading my Doritos in for two bottles of corner shop wine.

Dr. Burrowes told me that life after abuse is a bit like grief. It's something you learn to live with, and that process isn't easy. A lot of it has to do with striking a balance and slowly figuring out what you're comfortable with. What happened to you warrants all the compassion in the world; it's not an easy thing to get over. It's fucked up and it's catastrophically unfair, but many people can expect to fully recover from trauma.

On a good day it does help for me to put things into the context of my whole life. The assault isn't going to redefine everything I've been through so far, and it's not going to define what's yet to come.

5. You Aren't Obligated to Do Anything

After a sexual assault, you might feel it's important to report what's happened to you. There can be several motivations for this. The fact remains that reporting assault isn't easy—there's a tremendous amount of labor involved, which you're expected to carry out on top of the pressure of having to deal with trauma.

The criminal justice system expects the world from you. Make sure reporting your incident is absolutely what you want. If you want the person to face charges and you know that that process itself will be empowering to you, then it's a good move.

If possible, gather a good support network around you that has your back. You might need people to lift you up when it all gets overwhelming.

There are people who have reported their assault and had good experiences: they were listened to and ultimately they were vindicated. However, not everyone has the outcome they hoped for. The process is draining and will differ depending on what country you're in. If the assault happened recently, go to the police station as soon as possible and bring someone you trust. You might be examined for evidence, which can include saliva, blood, and urine samples. Photographs might be taken, and it's very likely you'll be encouraged to have a test for any sexually transmitted diseases.

6. Guilt Is a Coping Mechanism

I spent a lot of time flip-flopping between rage against the perpetrator and rage against myself. I told myself I probably led him on. I reminded myself of how drunk I can get, and I even concluded that even if it was rape, I probably deserved it anyway.

The guilt was relentless and exhausting, but what helped me climb out of it was the idea that guilt was a way for my brain to deal with the situation. Guilt, while detrimental to your feeling of self-worth, makes you feel like you had some kind of control. Guilt was giving me a power I didn't have, while also shielding me from the cold truth that callous people will ignore your boundaries, and there's nothing you can do about it.

This guilt mechanism is often seen among victims of child abuse. Children grow up believing they were to blame for their abuse, which is a slightly easier concept to process than the fact that people who are meant to protect you set out to hurt you. How can your young brain process something like that?

7. Communities Can Help

What's helped me immensely in accepting my mental health issues is talking to other people with similar experiences. The same can be said after you've experienced sexual assault. In a support group you get to see how other people are carrying the same baggage as you. You might also be able to contextualize some of the emotions you're struggling with by seeing other people grapple with them. Trauma is incredibly isolating, but getting together with other people can turn the table on your shame. In a group setting, I feel a flicker of power in my belly: "Look at us, we're sitting here, persisting, living our fucking lives despite the horrible things we've been through."

8. Dissociation Is Scary, but It's Not Unusual

I'll talk more about dissociation later in the book, but I experienced very acute dissociation before and after the incident. The MIND website describes dissociation as "an experience where you feel disconnected in some way from the world around you or from yourself."

Dissociation during a traumatic event happens frequently. Psychiatrist Bessel van der Kolk writes in *The Body Keeps the Score*: "Dissociation is the essence of trauma. The overwhelming experience is split off and fragmented, so that emotions, sounds, images, thoughts, and physical sensations related to the trauma take on a life of their own."

This fragmentation can occur at any point, during or after. I often feel like there's no way of knowing what might trigger it for me, even now, long after that evening. I might be in a pub having a Sunday roast when all of a sudden the back of my brain becomes a wardrobe I get sucked into. The other side isn't Narnia, it's a no-man's-land where snow has been.

While these episodes are scary, what helped me was normalizing what was happening and trying my hardest not to fight it. If I could feel that floaty feeling set in I'd try and talk to myself with compassion: "Something is triggering this. You feel unsafe. Remind yourself you're OK. You're doing fine."

I began to see my dissociative episodes as my brain trying to integrate my experience. I started to view my mind and body as one, rather than two conflicting entities. They want to coexist, they want to deal with what's happened to me, but they just struggle sometimes.

It was also helpful to stop trying to come up with a solution for everything that was happening. I'm one of those people who will run to Google whenever any kind of symptom occurs: "Why is my eye twitching and what can I do to stop it?" After trauma your mind is completely shattered; it needs time to heal. Not everything that happens to you has a solution. Sometimes your mind just needs a little rest. When you sprain your ankle, your body won't let you walk on that ankle. It hurts

> Sometimes your mind just needs a little rest.

because it wants a break; the pain is functional. In a similar way, my dissociation is functional too. It's telling me to give my mind a rest. Don't push it. Don't push myself. Take things one step at a time.

9. Not Everything You'll Do to Cope Will Be Good for You

As a self-harmer, I thought it made sense to self-harm after the assault. My self-harm was performing a function. I'd been using it as a coping mechanism for over half my life, why wouldn't I use it now? Yes, it's unhealthy and damaging, but now just wasn't the time to come up with a new plan. I had to resort to what I knew. I had to find some relief.

I also sought out sexual situations that weren't always right for me; I was trying to regain control by testing my limits. Perhaps part of me wanted to find out if all men were assholes. My body became a litmus test. If they stop when I tell them to, then they're OK.

10. People with Good Intentions May Still Say the Wrong Thing

On top of managing your own feelings, should you wish to tell people about what happened to you, you may have to manage theirs as well. Some of the most hurtful comments might be voiced by those who love you the most. People say things that subtly slut shame you or place the blame on you without meaning to. Even just a simple "Please be careful next time" implies that it was somehow your fault to begin with.

I think it's helpful to remember that people carry their own baggage with them wherever they go. When you share a story, they'll interpret it through the filter of their own experiences, and sometimes their response won't come out the right way.

Sometimes I fear that my boundaries are nonnegotiable, that I'll never learn to trust someone or let my guard down, but then I remember that they aren't physical things. They're not actual walls, they *can* become flexible and prone to change if you want them to and you're ready. Your boundaries can extend and pull back as much as you're comfortable with. They're there to keep others at a safe distance, but they allow you to choose whom to let into the space you might exclude others from. You're in control and you can change your mind whenever you want. Your boundaries are yours.

CHAPTER 10

Remember This When You're Losing Your Job

Keeping everything locked inside, hidden from view is a bad idea. I've known that since I was a kid. When I was bullied I'd swallow all the rage inside me, shut myself in my room, and just sit there. The rage had nowhere to go. I hated those kids, but I didn't do anything about it. I stored all that anger inside me until it began to turn on me: "This is your fault. They're right. You *are* dumb. You *are* fat."

That penchant for silence and bottling things up has cropped up in my work life as well, when the tasks keep piling up and everyone assumes I'm doing fine because I sit at my desk every day and I smile and say hi to people who walk past. In fact I've probably woken up that morning with *extreme* dread in my chest. I don't want to be at work. I don't think I can do it. I'm not cut out for this. I try and break my job down into little sections, but when it comes to lunch I can hear people talking but nothing goes in. A manager might check in on me and I say, "I'm fine," but meanwhile I feel like the room is spinning and I'm pretty sure my manager's head is slowly drifting off of her body. Things are really not fine.

One morning when I worked as a social media editor at BuzzFeed I'd reached a new limit. My levels of stress and exhaustion hit the summit. Instead of asking for help, calling in sick, seeing the doctor, or even picking myself up and getting through the day, my mind and my body said "enough!" They were finally working together, but not to my benefit.

I woke up and it was obvious: I wasn't going to go to work. I couldn't. I couldn't see the point. In fact, I couldn't see the point in blinking, breathing, or thinking. Nothing worked.

I lay on top of my duvet and tried to will dying on myself, I was too zombified to go out and kill myself, but I wished for a secret power where I could shut my eyes and end it all. What seemed like a few minutes of lying there turned into hours. I hadn't moved. In my head time was passing in slow motion, but in the real world things were ticking along as usual. My managers at work were naturally extremely worried. In fact, they'd even called the police to show up at my house. My family had been called. My ex-boyfriends. While I lay in bed trying to hold my breath, I'd caused complete and utter chaos around me. Around 3 p.m. that day, I took a deep breath and pushed my upper body upright to check my phone. By then it was too late. I couldn't go into work. I had well and truly fucked up.

As you might imagine, the aftermath wasn't good. Instead of using this opportunity to be honest, I opted for the usual: silence and sugarcoating. I blamed food poisoning and extreme tiredness. No one believed me. I told lie on top of lie and caused far more damage than I had to begin with.

When I told my BuzzFeed managers after things escalated and became much worse, I'd been suicidal for the past month, and naturally I was super distressed. I couldn't speak without crying. My skin was red and blotchy. My hands were shaking. I'd made a list of things to say when I approached them, but couldn't read the letters through tears. It's easy to think, "Oh, if only I'd told them about this sooner," but at the time I was very much in the present, it was happening, and I felt trapped. They told me I could go on an early lunch break, which I took eagerly and walked around Soho hoping to find something that would tell me what to do. My work building loomed in the background. I'd have to return at some point. I lit a cigarette and pressed it against my skin, but stopped before it made contact. I couldn't do this again. My scars had just healed. I'd only just stopped wearing my bandages. My cigarette hung suspended in midair. A group of beauticians came out on their own smoke break and I moved somewhere quieter. I couldn't stop thinking about harming myself. Every item on the street looked like a tool I could use: a piece of glass, a window I could smash, a bus I could jump in front of. My mind went into video game mode spotting ways to cause damage.

I took a breath and let a different part of my brain take over. It was a softer part, gentler; it was looking out for me. I still seemed to be in a video game, but in a different level altogether. This wasn't about hurting myself anymore; I needed to get help. I needed to get to the ER. I texted work I couldn't come back and went into the ER, using a voice that seemed to come from some alien part of my body, saying I was worried I was going to hurt myself. That I'd been seen here before for self-harm wounds and I didn't think I was safe in my own company.

I felt like I wasn't me anymore. I was just a hollow bit of flesh, handing myself over to someone else's care. They looked after me, transferred me to a mental health unit, and released me in the evening. There weren't any beds available and I managed to convince them I was going to be OK. I had a friend's house I could stay in. I'd see my counselor the next day, and to be honest, at this point, I was just too tired to do anything self-destructive.

The following week I came back to work carrying a massive load of shame with me. Thanks to the support of a few colleagues who were aware of my mental health issues, I decided to finally tell the truth. I hadn't been doing well, I hadn't been looking after myself, and my mental health was faltering. I wasn't fired, but I was given an official warning, and in what ended up being a great result, my employers took some steps to make sure that not just mine, but other people's mental health would be better supported in the office.

I should've felt relieved that I still had a job, but I was still so desperately ashamed. Going into work was even harder than it had been before. I felt marked. I felt like I'd let everyone down. Then, to my surprise, a more senior colleague took me to lunch. He's a very clever and talented writer and editor I'd always looked up to. He had dark hair, a beard, and always carried a fancy umbrella and a book whose title I'd scribble down in secret to make sure I read it too. I knew that he ran (and continues to run) a support group for people with bipolar disorder who work in the media. I'd spoken to him in the pub once vaguely about my issues, and I think he saw straight through my deflections and jokes that maybe I needed help. When I'd come back from work after a few days of absence he asked if I was free.

We went to a Korean restaurant near Oxford Circus. I tried to be happy and grateful that someone so senior wanted to spend his lunch with me. I wanted to ask him about some of the features he'd edited, career highlights, etc. I didn't want to talk about my fuckups, I didn't want to launch into some kind of dramatic monologue about how much I'd messed up my career, but I took one bite of my kimchi and blurted everything out. He listened and said two things that I'll never, ever forget.

1. It's just a job.
   "Yes you fucked up," he said. "But ultimately it's just a job. You can find a new one." I know this seems bizarrely simple, but so much of my identity was tied up into this role and making it work—without it I didn't know who I was. If I was fired, how would I pay my rent? How would I eat? What else could I possibly do?

   _____

   You need to become your own advocate.

   _____

2. You need to become your own advocate. "You have to be your own carer, because if you don't do it, no one else will."

When you have a mental illness that impacts your daily life, you not only have to deal with the fallout from that, you also have to be there to clean it up, to defend yourself, to tell everyone this is not your fault. When you need support you have to go out there and get the help you need. You have to call various mental health services and get yourself an appointment. If they're fully booked, don't give up. Ring someone else. Try another service. You have to keep going. It's important. I knew this, but part of me was waiting for someone else to save me. Someone who'd swoop in and do all the calling and organizing for me, but at that point I'd alienated so many people it was really just me, by myself. I had to get myself better.

From that lunch on I tried to be better at being my own advocate. If I needed a day off from work because depression was crushing my skull I'd ask for it. If I needed to see my GP again to up my SSRI dosage, I'd give them a ring, and another ring if they were busy. I arranged to have another psych assessment, as the others were inconclusive, which was a massive headache to reschedule. I did it anyway. I had to.

When you're starting out in a new job, it's so hard to figure out how much you should disclose about your mental health. The bottom line for me has always been, considering the job market is a bit of a shitshow, I've always been grateful to even have a job, and I'd rather not fuck it up.

Bad mental health isn't fucking up though. In the UK, a lot of conditions are protected from work discrimination under the Equality Act. The act isn't there to tell you you're not normal or good enough to join the team. It's there to protect you when you're afraid your mental health is costing you your career.

There's a societal failure at present in adjusting for mental illness at work. Whereas in the past I've had no issue calling in sick because I have the flu, I've dragged my depressed body to work a number of times. It was only when I became honest about my situation that I was able to manage my work balance far better. I made a list of what I needed from work, which wasn't a lot. I needed to leave early on Wednesdays to make it to therapy, and I needed to work from home on occasion if my anxiety or OCD had flared up. The more specific you are about your requests, and why you're making them, the better. For example, my medication can make me feel quite groggy, so working ten to six is better for me than nine to five, as I can make sure my mind is alert before I start the day. I've worked in big open-plan offices that would give the most rational person a dose of anxiety, so I like the freedom of being able to move to a quieter room (usually an empty meeting room) so the noise doesn't make my brain whizz around.

Some workplaces make it easier to ask for these adjustments than others. When I joined the BBC, I was amazed at all the flyers and posters advertising mental health support and helplines and people you could talk to. It made approaching my own managers that much easier.

It's up to you when you decide to tell your employer about any of your conditions, but from my experience the earlier on the better. If you wait till you're in the midst of something and crisis has struck, you might not be as articulate as you'd like. Things might get emotional and complicated. There's also a chance your employers will feel misled: "Why didn't she tell us about this before?"

Then of course there is the off chance that despite all the precautions you have in place, something boils up and *boom*, you can't sit through a single meeting without welling up. Whether it's your mental health or your situation, sometimes you need to be able to let loose.

Here's how I've dealt with secret breakdowns at work:

- Go outside and stomp around the building. Go without a coat so you feel the cold. Scream into the wind.

- Don't apologize if you're crying; you're allowed to cry and be emotional, and there's nothing wrong with that.

- Go to the disabled loo (but make sure you're not hogging it from someone who actually needs it, as that's just dickish), go into fetal position on the floor, pop a hoodie over your face, and just pretend you're somewhere else for a bit

- Punch the air really fast. Clench your fists and keep punching.

- Arrange something fun to do after work so you know the second time is up you can bust out of there and do something more interesting

- Google other jobs (on the sly) that either you can apply for later or just to remind yourself that a job is just a job and you can get another one, it's fine

- Walk back to your desk and put your headphones on. Play "I Will Survive" and get back to whatever you were doing for the remainder of the day.

- Come in the next day dressed as a fucking queen, power suit and all

CHAPTER 11

Remember This
When You're Alone

When work and the wider world get too overwhelming, I seek my own company more than anyone else's. I see solitude as a warm bath. I love it. I love sitting in it for hours, enjoying the warm water enveloping my entire body. Only thing is, despite how much I love it when I'm in it, I struggle with the idea of it. A bath is just a stew of your own filth. Solitude is just you and your own filth because no one else wants in.

There are different shades of aloneness. It's not as simple as occupying a space without anyone else. It's multilayered and complex. I might have the house to myself for the week, enjoying the comfort of being a slob, not tidying up, singing out loud. And then there's a point where the loneliness piles up like a stack of dirty dishes. The stack gets higher and higher until it topples over and my room is littered with sad bits of ceramic.

There are types of isolation that make me feel uncomfortable. They are a different shade, darker, heavier, and more restrictive. There's a self-imposed loneliness that's often a form of self-protection. People tend to experience this after a loss, whether it's a breakup or a loved one passing. In the midst of your grief, human contact seems unbearable. You put yourself in an isolation cell of your own making. It feels easier because the outside world operates at a different pace. They're not experiencing what you are; they are lost to you. No matter how many people offer to hold your hand, you're still achingly alone. You can't pass your grief around like a cigarette. It's yours to get through.

It's important to give yourself space while also giving yourself permission to be happy again, because loneliness as a form of self-punishment is dangerous. You fold in on yourself. When I was a student, I banished myself to the confines of my flat. I exiled myself from the student union, the pubs, and societies because I didn't think anyone would like me. Why would they? I was boring, dumb, lifeless. Why should I subject anyone else to that? I retreated so far into my exile that when a flicker of hope of genuine friendship arose, I didn't make any effort. It was so much easier to give in to the voices and agree, "Yeah, they'll probably just hate me anyway," than to follow up and actually take a chance.

There was also an anxiety that befriending someone would tie me into a binding contract. What if they wanted me to meet up all the time? What if they wanted me to go clubbing or do drugs? What if they wanted to stay over? What if I couldn't live up to their expectations? What if they never left me alone? It's incredibly frustrating when you've mentally entangled yourself to such an extent that a simple thing such as friendship seems like a bad idea. Why make the effort? Just go back to bed. Things are easier there.

Depression and anxiety often carry with them a loneliness that cages you in; you're locked in with no place to go.

It's a loneliness that's never subtle or passive. Instead it snaps at you, barks, and chomps at your feet wherever you go. Even if you're in the middle of a crowd or surrounded by people who care about you, you still feel totally cut off. That feeling can be so visceral for me that I actually feel as if I'm taking up less space. I'm slowly disappearing. Everyone else's connectedness seems to mock how hollow my life feels. I hear teenage girls gossiping on the Tube and feel jealous. I see bartenders sharing a joke before a shift and wish I could join in. Why don't I have that? Why am I not bonded to anyone?

Another type of loneliness I experienced growing up stemmed from the fact that some of my most meaningful relationships were happening online. At fourteen, I shied away from real friends and turned to friends I found on forums, where often quite self-destructive people came together to share details of their lives (more on these forums later).

To me these friendships were as real as the flesh-and-blood variety. We shared intimate details of our lives, what we'd had to eat, what music we listened to, who we were annoyed with that day. We shared lyrics and poetry and offered help and advice when we could. For me, these relationships added an element to my life that wasn't there: people to check in with. However, it took away my chance to build these connections in the real world—in school for example. My social skills faltered as I continually ran home to go on my computer and talk to women who were ten years older than me living far, far away. If I couldn't wait till then, I'd go to the library at lunch and log in on the computers there.

I don't have these online friendships anymore. I deleted my forum accounts when I was twenty. The pull of cyber companionship never waned, but it was more important for me to build a life outside of my computer screen. Forums gave me an excuse to disengage from reality. I'll never be someone with a massive group of friends, but I have wonderful people in my life I love to see one on one. I share things with them, I confide in them, and they help me grow as a person.

For me, loneliness requires a balancing act. It's not all doom and gloom. As an introvert I crave the space to fill my head with my own thoughts. I enjoy thinking out loud. I enjoy talking out loud. I enjoy not having to communicate with anyone else. What keeps solitude at a level I'm comfortable with is that I know should I wish to go back to the "real world," I have the option to engage with someone, whether it's via phone or in person. My loneliness won't swallow me up. There's an expiration date. There's someone on the other end of the phone.

I also like knowing exactly what I'm going to do with alone time. It's not extended out in front of me like an African desert. I can visualize what I want to do, what I want to read and listen to. These activities can be unproductive. They'll probably include finding new golden retriever Instagram accounts to follow or making a spreadsheet of shoes I'd like to buy once I'm rich. I try not to judge myself when I'm alone.

I like to make sure I eat and drink enough, and that I'm not surrounded by self-harm tools. It's important I make sure my solitude doesn't become an act of self-destruction like it used to. And every day I'm still proving that I can take care of myself. That I can use my me time as an opportunity to be healthy and happy rather than miserable and reclusive.

> I try not to judge myself when I'm alone.

Alone at home is one thing, then there's being alone in motion, when you're out and about. There aren't any clean sheets I can swaddle myself in, but I enjoy it all the same. I like wandering by myself with a vague sense of purpose, toward a goal that doesn't have a timed deadline: maybe a park or an exhibition. I try to walk at a slower pace when I'm doing this, not that fast trot I do when I'm rushing to work and my bags are flailing around the place.

When you're comfortable with your own company, I highly recommend taking yourself on a date. It's something people are constantly recommending in women's magazines, and it feels cheesy, but I really do recommend it. A cinema is easy, you can hide in the darkness. A fancy meal can be trickier, but it's equally fulfilling. I like my own company in a restaurant. I like thinking about things, slowly, unhurried. I like ordering just for me. I like not having to come up with things to talk about and I like not having to worry if someone reaches for their phone. My social tics and stresses are shushed. I'm there for myself, with myself. There's no pressure.

I've taken myself to lots of different places: McDonald's, fancy French restaurants, diners, service station cafés, cosmopolitan bars, Mars-themed sports bars, Dutch bars abroad—most bars to be honest.

Whether like me you'd like to have a great date in McDonald's, or you're thinking of something a little more upmarket, here are some things you might find useful:

- Don't worry about anyone staring at you. On the whole, people are too wrapped up in their own lives to notice other people. Even when I have spotted someone eating alone, I never thought they were lame or sad: if anything I was envious.
- If being seen alone is still a worry for you, you can go for a table in the corner rather than sit in the middle of the room. I like sitting by the window so I can look out at the world and I don't feel too enclosed.
- Bring a book or a newspaper, or another form of entertainment. There's no one at your table telling you you're being rude. I once saw a guy in Pizza Express eating on his own while he kicked back with a glass of wine, some dough balls, and an episode of The Wire on his laptop. Goals.
- Bring a notepad. When I eat alone I like to make notes. These aren't super profound Aristotelian observations, but they might be little descriptions of people or some material for

poetry or a short story I'll get to later. It's nice to give myself the space to sit, enjoy food someone else made, and be creative.

- Eavesdrop as much as you like. It's possibly the best perk about eating alone: listening to other people's conversations. You might hear an awkward first date, coworkers gossiping about their boss, or two old friends making amends after a fall out.

- Along with eavesdropping, you can people watch as much as you like. Where I'm from in the Netherlands it's all about terrace life. Most bars and restaurants have an outside section where the chairs face the street. You're all gazing in the same direction, watching people walk and cycle past. If you can, opt for a terrace, sit there for hours.

- Pay attention to what you're eating. Order things that are bursting with flavor: rich pasta sauces, bitter coffee, velvety red wine. Roll the ingredients around your tongue, dig your teeth in, and relish the food you've treated yourself to.

- Don't feel like you have to chat with anyone. The best thing for me about bars in the UK is that bartenders rarely strike up a conversation. At most, they'll ask what I'm reading or whether I want another drink. When I went to New York by myself I did a lot of sitting at a bar with a book, and the bartenders would not stop chatting. Some of them were dashing and charming and had relatively interesting stories to tell. Others would fill me in on their fantasy football league or pass judgment on my choice of drink. I've learned

to be quite cutthroat if someone is talking to me and I'm not in the mood. It's perfectly OK to put your head back down and delve back into your book. I've been overly polite for most of my life; it's time to let a few things go. If I'm reading and you're telling me my choice of white wine is unrefined, you can piss off.

■ If you're not comfortable taking yourself out to a restaurant just yet, start with smaller activities and then build on them. Go farther away from home, go for longer, and eventually, when you're ready, go on an adventure.

At a point where my mental health was teetering over the edge of "Houston, we have a problem," I decided to leave London. I found an extraordinarily cheap Eurostar ticket

and a tiny Airbnb studio I could stay in for 20 euros a night right by Père Lachaise.

My trip got off to a rocky start (as these solo ventures sometimes do), but waking up on the second day in Paris, I updated my Spotify playlist and decided to set out on a wander with no real purpose. I walked and walked, and only checked Google Maps about an hour in. I took photos. I ate a croissant and sang along to Fiona Apple in my earphones. I felt like I was in a movie, but in a filler scene: this wasn't advancing the plot, I was simply just being.

When my legs began to ache I figured out my way home going through the famous Père Lachaise cemetery. I'd been there before, so I didn't get stressed out about having to find Oscar Wilde's or Jim Morrison's tombstone. I was the most relaxed and the most present I'd felt in months. I'd given up on my frantic search for connection. I didn't feel lonely any-more. I felt at peace, letting my body move in whichever di-rection it wanted to.

When I went back to Britain, I still had a lot of shit to deal with, Brexit being one of them, but I kept up this new form of walking I'd learned. Walking without a clear purpose has led me to discover beautiful places in London: marshes and hills and mews and lavender fields. And I've gone further afield. I've been hiking in Hastings and Essex, and I've taken myself on romantic beach walks on the south coast. I've learned that I'm not bad company; I'm all right, and the more I can let go the better I am as a travel buddy. I've learned to stop looking for a connection elsewhere and to start trying to connect the frag-mented bits within myself.

Here's what I learned on my solo excursions:

- Figure out your traveling style and commit to it. Whether I'm traveling alone or with someone, I like to build an itinerary. I do my research before and I like to get excited about some of the things I'm going to see. My old housemate Virginie is a keen solo traveler, but her style is totally different. She makes sure she's packed enough clothes, has enough foreign currency, and one night's accommodation on the day she arrives. She'll also allow herself to buy one guidebook that she won't open until she's on the plane traveling to her destination. This is how she travels and she thrives doing it. She's been to Nepal, Burma, and Mexico, and likes to be surprised and steered by her own spontaneous curiosity. It's the thing I love about her the most, but it's absolutely not for me.

- Figure out what the things are that make you stressed when traveling and plan ahead. Get the visa sorted, travel insurance, and a physical map in case you're like me and your phone is constantly dying.

- Don't be afraid to approach people. If you need to ask for directions or you want to find a good place to eat, open your mouth and strike up a conversation. Start small if you're nervous: maybe ask a receptionist where the closest ATM is, or ask your Airbnb host where the best breakfast spot is.

- If you want to be alone but not completely alone, you can meet other solo travelers by staying in hostels, guest houses, or community-run accommodation. You could even travel with a small-group tour company that gives you the option to make friends.

- There are lots of Facebook groups and online networks you can join for the area you'll be traveling to, which will help you figure out what you want to do when you get there (or even plan a meetup and make a friend).

- Schedule a regular check-in with people back home. It's nice for them to know you're still alive, and it's comforting knowing someone is keeping an eye out for you. If your friends and family tend to worry about you, stick to a prearranged time: e.g., every other day at 7 p.m. so you don't have to waste time finding a right time in different time zones or getting your phone to work while you're on top of a mountain.

- This might sound a bit childish, but it works for a lot of people. If you find yourself getting a bit stressed while you're off on your own somewhere, it can help to start talking to yourself as a "we." The other person can be an invisible partner, a friend, or just another you. Using an imaginary we gives you a sense of companionship and security. I often change between a "we" and a "you"—the you comes from the other me that's cheering the actual me along. So when I made my train back from Paris when I thought I was about to miss it, I said (out loud even): "Well done, you did it!"

- Don't feel like you have to say yes to everything. Even if you're embarking on your own version of *Eat Pray Love* and you want to experience everything, you don't have to be spontaneous 24/7. You're allowed to say no to some things. If you want to have a nap, have that nap. If you want to go to McDonald's instead of a hyperlocal street food café, you're allowed to. Don't put pressure on yourself, trust your instincts, and listen to your gut: what do you really want to do?

CHAPTER 12

Remember This When You're Online

One way to travel and explore without really having to leave your bed is to log on to your computer. Online you can witness sights and sounds and different people. It's easy to feel a sense of community. The internet can be a place where you can find a hub of support with wonderful people giving great advice, but it's also a hotbed of self-loathing, loudmouthed trolls, and self-destructive clubs.

I don't envy teens who grow up today, with the internet wrapped around wherever they go. I was teased in school. I hid in gym toilets and beneath staircases to get away from the chanting. The greatest escape would come when it was time to go home again. There was no more invasion of words and pokes and trip-ups; no one would get me when I was holed up in my room. Now with social media the bullying never stops. You go home, log on, and it starts all over again. People have pictures and videos. It's impossible to feel safe.

Even if you don't have to deal with bullies, the internet is filled with booby traps of upsetting content. There are articles, videos, images begging for your click. Even if a publication doesn't aim to cause you any harm, just reading about self-harm or seeing scars might ignite the urge within you. Eating disorder recovery stories in tabloids always get to me. The focus is never on how healthy the person is now, it's on how sick they once were. They splash images of bones and feeding tubes trying to shock you. It's less about the well-being of the person they're writing about and more about enticing the body horror fantasy within the reader.

I have to approach the internet with care. Every couple of days I fall into a YouTube hole where I have to text my boyfriend and he comes to my rescue—usually by taking the phone out of my hand. After a tough day recently, I went to the pub and embarked on a three-hour YouTube expedition into videos about the Manson murders. As the pub grew darker, I became less conscious of my surroundings, clicking on a new clip as soon as the current clip had ended. I was getting more and more upset. I felt horrified for the victims, the young women who had been indoctrinated by the cult, and even Charles Manson, who'd experienced a childhood of rape and abuse.

When it was finally time to leave the pub, I was drained, zombielike, and my eyes twitched from the hyperfocus strain I'd put on them. And this situation wasn't a one-time thing for me. The internet feels infinite; once I start reading troubling material, I will keep going, even if it's upsetting me. Even if there's a big trigger warning splashed across something, I'll click it, just to see what it is. "It can't be that bad," I'll think—and it always is.

While I can't approach the internet with gloves on, I can identify the places I know will hurt me mentally. The internet is vast, but there are little patches I know I need to avoid. Here are some of them:

PRO-ANA COMMUNITIES

There's a dark, cultlike corner of the internet, which used to reside mostly on LiveJournal and Xanga, that attracts people from all over the world who seem intent on starving themselves.

Pro-ana (pro-anorexia) and pro-mia (pro-bulimia) are terms

used by people who talk about eating disorders like they're a lifestyle choice instead of the crippling mental disorders they are. Members of pro-ana groups exchange tips, "thin commandments," and "thinspiration" to motivate one another to continue dieting, bingeing, and purging.

I first joined a pro-ana community when I was thirteen. I had been given a writing assignment about eating disorders and female representation in the media. Coincidentally, I was also given a drama assignment to create a five-minute play about bulimia.

While I was doing research for these projects I read an article condemning pro-ana communities on Xanga and LiveJournal. The article said these forums were a threat to young girls and needed to be shut down. I had never heard of pro-ana before. I decided to stop reading about it and experience the whole thing myself. I made an account, gave myself a fake name, and dove in.

As I read back my own LiveJournal entries, they don't feel like me. I was trying to copy the pro-ana mindset, own it, and eventually adopt it, which I did. Pro-ana women were angsty, angry, and insecure, and I found comfort in that. That was how I felt on the inside, even before I hated my body.

Partaking in their challenges gave me a sense of purpose and control. There was a group where they'd set a calorie limit for the day, and whoever stuck to it the most "won." You didn't win anything apart from admiration from your fellow group members, which for people who were social misfits in their real life meant everything.

The first groups I joined had names like "anaXcore" and "proed_bones," and have since been deleted or changed into "pro-recovery" communities. Membership required you to post stats and a brief history of your experience with bingeing and purging. For me, that was pretty hardcore. I lurked, almost admiring the dedication, but not wanting to tell a stick-thin teenager that she should "keep going." Some group members would post naked photos of themselves and invite critique: "You could probably do with losing some weight on your hips," or, "Your collarbones would look cute if they're more pronounced." These comments were people's own eating disorders talking, and who could blame them? We live in a society where female bodies are constantly scrutinized, even policed. These pro-ana members had perfected the art of scrutiny.

While the pro-ana group offered me a refuge from my depression, isolation, and aimlessness, it taught me how to be mean. Not to other people, but to myself.

I did make friends on LiveJournal. There was a group of older women that took me in as their virtual younger sister. We stopped talking about food and dieting, and they helped me with my homework, introduced me to Sylvia Plath and Elliott Smith and Fiona Apple. I genuinely owe the discovery of a lot of the music and literature that shaped me to those women.

Unfortunately though, those friendships didn't come without a cost. We could send each other songs, but we couldn't save each other. I had to delete my account a few times, as my mum or a boyfriend found them, but I could never tell my online friends what had happened. We were constantly stressed when people didn't log on. Some women were absent because they had to go to rehab or they were committed. One woman I cared about greatly posted a final piece of writing about how she'd gone off the rails and descended back into her crystal meth addiction. I still think about that woman every day. I never knew her real name or where exactly she lived. I have no way of knowing if she's OK.

These types of communities come in all shapes and sizes. When I shared my pro-ana stories with my first housemate in London, she told me she'd joined something similar as a teen, but it was about self-harm. She told me they'd post photos of their cuts in forums, and share tips on how to cut deeper and how to hide the wounds from their parents. She's spent the same amount of time in those groups as I had in mine. I loved her, and still think she's one of the most wonderful women I've ever met, but she doesn't know that herself and can't accept it. That dangerously cruel voice she honed on those sites, telling her she deserved all that self-inflicted pain, is still with her today, telling her she's worthless.

If you put a bunch of scared, lonely, and self-destructive people together, you can't expect them to be equipped with the right tools to help each other out.

TROLL COMMENTS

As an adult using the internet now, you might not have bullies you know personally attacking you online, but you have to deal with trolls. Those are people who sit in dark rooms spewing out their own personal agenda in comments and tweets, tearing anyone down who stands in their way.

A study by communications professor Stine Eckert concluded that 73.4 percent of women who blog or post about feminism, family, and/or maternity politics on their social media accounts receive abusive comments, stalking, trolls, rape threats, death threats, and unpleasant off-line encounters.

I once wrote an article with the sarcastic title of "21 Reasons You Should Never Visit the Netherlands." It was a style of headline that BuzzFeed used a lot at the time. It drives people's curiosity, and once they click, they realize the page is filled with reasons the country is actually beautiful. Simple, right? Well, I still get messages from people who never bothered to click. They send them to my Facebook and Twitter accounts and my personal email. They tell me I'm a bitch, a whore, that it's good I don't live in Holland, that they should take away my passport, that I don't deserve my nationality. I used to reply asking them to actually read the damn thing, but I've stopped now—there's no point.

The best way to deal with trolls is to ignore them, but that seems like you're backing down or hiding away. Platforms like Facebook and Twitter are flawed in that they're not very good at protecting their users from abuse, but it's still important to report people who send you things that make you feel unsafe.

GOOGLE

It's a bit unfair to claim that Google is bad for my mental health. On the whole it isn't, but it is incredibly easy to use Google to make my hypochondria thrive. From convincing myself I'm pregnant with a demon baby made of fingernails to thinking I have syphilis and meningitis at the same time, my Google searches send me into a pit of despair.

While Google has helped me find solace in anxiety forums where people talk about their panic attacks and other symptoms, what became problematic was that reading about panic attacks tended to bring one on. I'd be trying to find comfort in other people's posts about how they too didn't get through their bus journey either, but when I read about their shortness of breath, dizziness, and hot flashes, my body seemed to mimic everything I was reading.

I think these forums are fantastic, but when you're still in a place where you're hypersensitive and you wear your triggers on your sleeve, you have to be careful you don't drown in a research avalanche.

When I was diagnosed with borderline personality disorder, I felt very comfortable with my diagnosis. I'd been reading about it for years; I read scientific journals and psychology magazines, and I have a great therapist who will point me in the right reading direction. However, when you Google a diagnosis with no prior knowledge of what it actually is, you can get sucked into accusatory and inaccurate articles.

When my boyfriend told me he was reading up about my personality disorder, I typed it into Google to see how the articles would look from his point of view. The third one Google suggested was called "Why You Should Never Date Girls with BPD." Granted, the article was hosted on an alt-right website, so I should've expected it really, but it was so hurtful to even see that title pop up. When you're using the internet in search of comfort, you have to remember there's a lot of thorns in your way. Don't take everything you read seriously.

> Don't take everything you read seriously.

INSTAGRAM

There are so many great communities on Instagram—take the body positive movement for example. It exists solely to connect people, spread self-love, and combat societal pressures. However, there's a part of Instagram that makes me feel inadequate, no matter how much my feed is filled with badass women, golden retrievers, and toddlers dressed like superheroes.

In a recent UK Snapchat survey, Instagram was rated the worst social platform when it comes to young people's mental health. People aged fourteen to twenty-four complained that the app caused a whole host of issues, including loneliness, depression, bullying, and negative body image.

The platform thrives off people's cleverly curated lives and pushes those lives right into our feeds. My vacation will never look as good as someone else's, and someone else will always have the very thing I want, whether it's a stable relationship, purple hair, or that new book everyone's raving about.

When I'm in a good place I use Instagram for inspiration. I'll save posts of fun places to eat in my neighborhood or cheap European cities I want to explore. When I'm in a bad place, Instagram is a gateway drug to self-doubt. I'll lurk on the profiles of three different ex-boyfriends, three women I think are intimidating, and sometimes I'll even trawl my own profile judging it like I'm the Simon Cowell of social media.

I have another Instagram-related habit that is absolutely detrimental and perhaps the ultimate form of social media self-sabotage: the unfollower app. Three times a year I allow myself to download an app that tells me who has unfollowed me on Instagram. Every time I imagine it'll be a fun exercise: "Oh look, that spambot unfollowed me," or "Oh, that blogger who probably thought I was more interesting unfollowed me," or, "My ex-boyfriend's mum has finally deleted me, har-har-har." Thing is, each time I allow myself to use this app, there's always something that bothers me a little bit too much and I get caught in a spiral of self-hatred.

I once found out that a former manager of mine who I always looked up to as being a very cool, savvy woman with all the business smarts in the world had pressed the unfollow button on my account. She still followed everyone else we'd both worked with (I double-checked, but I hadn't made the cut). I should have shrugged and moved on, but I became mildly obsessed with this. I was tempted to phone her up to ask if she'd made a mistake (thank god I didn't follow through with this). I then looked at my account through the eyes of my friends and concluded there must be something terribly off-putting about my posts. Maybe I post too frequently? Maybe my captions are too rude? Maybe my filters are too garish?

I thought about deleting my account for a second until I stepped back and thought about how extreme my behavior was at this point. It's a social media platform, it's not real life, chill out! I've started to use Instagram in a healthier way.

I've unfollowed "hate follows" (the people you actually dislike but you follow to have a good sneak peek at their lives), and I've limited my lurking on people's profiles to twice a week (nobody's perfect). Here are some other ways I've made my account more mental health safe:

- Find your community: Instagram can be a friendly, supportive place if you surround yourself with the right people. If you have a hobby or a cause you particularly care about, fill your feed with those followers. I'm part of a Facebook group for female writers in London, and someone posted on their Instagram account wondering if people wanted to connect there. I jumped in and added about a hundred new people who were all similar to me: they loved books and writing and writing about books. My Instagram feed became less of a source of worry and more one of inspiration and camaraderie.

- You don't have to be brutally honest, but don't feel like you have to make your account picture perfect all the time. Unless your goal is to become an influencer with a gazillion followers, you can be relaxed about what you post. Granted, I'm not comfortable posting a selfie of me in the ER when I'm getting my second-degree burns treated, but I might post a picture of a crowded concert and how I was trying to ward off an anxiety attack. Doing this, I've connected with lots of other people who often post about their anxiety, and it helps us to be supportive of each other.

- Every now and again go on an Instagram detox. Step back and do an audit of everyone you follow. Does that friend who always bangs on about their yoga routine make you feel lazy and useless? Maybe get rid of them? You can also go into your settings and ban certain words from your comments in case you often get sucked into long comment threads you'd rather not be part of.

- Get a face-editing app. Seriously, once I got myself the Facetune app, I realized how easy it is to make your face look slimmer, more refined, and glowing. Even all those Snapchat filters give you dog ears, but they also sneakily make you look less pale. The reason everyone looks so banging on Instagram is because they've added an effect or two. I never actually posted a Facetuned creation of mine, apart from the time I posted a photo my sister took of me where my arms are up and I blurred out a nasty shaving rash on my armpit. It didn't really work, because I just ended up with a blurry pit, but still. It taught me that if you're better skilled at certain apps you could use it to all sorts of effect. The more you realize how airbrushed a lot of your Instagram faves are, the more you can put it into perspective. They put a lot of effort into looking that hot. If you can be bothered, great, and if not, stop worrying about it. It's not real.

INTERNET STALKING

Everyone looks up everyone else online. My first ever boyfriend and I became good friends after we broke up and he told me about a fight he was having with his new girlfriend. Apparently he'd seen that she checked my Instagram, Twitter, Facebook, and poetry Tumblr (hope she enjoyed my lack of iambic pentameter) most mornings before she got out of bed. He told her to stop doing it, but it had been so routine for her she didn't want to give it up.

Instead of being a bit freaked out by this, it actually made me want to run to her house to give her a massive hug and tell her I'd been stalking her just as much. I'd seen every inch of her life that existed online, from her Facebook page to her acting showreel to her vintage jewelry account on Etsy. There was nothing she'd put online that I hadn't seen. The fact that some-one was doing that level of snooping on me, a totally boring average individual, seemed ridiculous. She deserved to be stalked. She was an actress, she had long ginger hair like a mermaid, she liked Kanye—she was *perfect*. I wanted to con-nect with her and say, "Look, it's OK, I'm not very interesting, stop wasting your mornings on my accounts. Go live your life!" That's not how it works though. Instead we keep our heads down and convince ourselves that everyone else is better.

Whether you're dealing with trolls or bullies or your ex flaunting their new happy life, the internet is a mind fuck. For me, it's become incredibly important to treat the internet like a garden I've planted. I want the good things to grow and I want to get rid of the weeds. I've cultivated a place I feel safe. A place that makes me learn and a place that makes me laugh. Here's how:

- Engage with charities and organizations you care about. I found a charity that helps fight period poverty and they supply tampons and sanitary pads to women refugees who can't afford them. I started following them, helping out as a volunteer and getting other people on board too.
- Use your skills to do something useful. I started helping out with the social media feeds of a great charity in London that teaches young women to play musical instruments. I

spent time getting the word out there, designing assets, and attracting influencers who could help out.

- Find comfort in Facebook groups, as long as you don't find talking about mental health to be triggering. I'm part of twenty-five and counting Facebook groups. I love them. They make my Facebook usage more personal. Of those, ten are mental health groups, from Women with Anxiety to Women on the Borderline (you guessed it: a group for women with borderline personality disorder). You can use it to share some of the things you're struggling with or to celebrate the small, everyday victories that people without mental health issues might not understand.
- I also set up my own group called Women & Mental Health, where members share articles about mental health issues that got it either extremely right or extremely wrong, and we engage in a friendly discussion about that.
- Mental health communities on Twitter are great too. Twitter can feel like an endless stream of humblebrags or self-deprecation or both, but there are also lots of activists, spokespeople, and those who are dedicated to breaking down stigma.
- I post anonymously about my mental health struggles on sub-Reddits on Reddit. I've made some friends there, and we now use a shared app so we can chat about our therapy, relationship issues, and triggers on a daily basis.

■ Online support communities like Big White Wall and 7 Cups are great mental health resources too.

Remember this when you're getting help:

■ Don't try and tackle your mental health issue by yourself. It's important to confide in someone. It can feel hard to talk about what's going on in your mind. It feels like you're oversharing or causing a scene about nothing. But before you send yourself into a shame spiral keep these things in mind, because it's not at all weird to talk about mental health. Trust me.

■ At least one in four of us experiences mental health issues

■ By 2030, it is estimated that there will be approximately two million more adults in the UK with mental health problems than there were in 2013

■ Young women are the most at risk for mental health issues; more than *a third* of young women in Britain have reported feeling unhappy or worthless

■ Keeping your problems a secret makes it seem like they're your fault

■ Keeping mental health issues a secret makes it seem like this type of thing is incredibly uncommon (they're not: hello—one in four!)

■ The world can't see inside your mind: you have to tell them about it

> Talking is the quickest way to show someone you're in pain.

- Talking is the quickest way to show someone you're in pain
- No one should be made to feel like they have to hide any part of themselves
- Asking for help is important
- Asking for help might save your life
- You wouldn't find it strange to talk about a broken leg, so why should a broken brain be any different?
- Mentally ill people are not *a danger to society* as many headlines, TV shows, and films will have you believe
- Talking can be a lot like slowly letting air out of a balloon that's about to burst inside of you
- Friendships will grow stronger the more honest you are
- Relationships will never work if you shut yourself off
- The people who judge mental health conditions are the people you don't want to be around you anyway
- In sharing your struggles you're letting someone know they can come to you if they find themselves in a similar position
- Being vulnerable can make you stronger

I've always yearned for close friendships. I've learned that there's no blueprint for them. Everyone has different needs and expectations. At least by never belonging to a big group of people, I've never experienced the negative sides either: the falling-outs and other dramas. Perhaps a group would never have suited me anyway. Maybe I would fade into the background or constantly go along with whatever everyone else wants to do?

I've learned it's quality over quantity when it comes to friendships. In a group setting I find myself trying extra hard to fit in (unless I find Scrabble aficionados). One on one, I know the friend likes me enough to hang out with me. I don't have to be someone else, someone different. One on one I know I can take up my friend's time and attention, which means it's easier to talk openly about anything I might be dealing with.

Telling someone about your mental health is daunting but important. It can mean that you dispel some of that heavy fog inside you. You're letting someone in, even if it's just a tiny bit, and it stops you from becoming isolated. Putting up a front and convincing people that I'm actually 100 percent OK requires a lot of smoke screens. I have to overdo any good news I conjure up for myself just to make it sound believable: "Oh yes, met up with that girl from work, it was great, so, so great! Had a really great, great time! Everything's great!" Even just looking at my Instagram during one of my lowest periods a year ago, I can see a lot of photos of me at parties in pubs, looking like I'm having a great time, but with key give-aways: a bandage wrapped around my arm from elbow to wrist and eyes that are carrying the weight of three weeks' worth of crying.

Why telling your friends about how you're feeling is a good idea:

- You are not a burden. At their core people are good and they want to help each other, they just don't always know how to. Think about how you feel when someone comes to you asking for advice. I genuinely feel useful and even a slight bit honored, and I need to get it into my head that it's the same the other way around.

- You don't have to do everything by yourself. Battling a mental health problem, whether it's temporary or more permanent, is something that requires help. You need backup. Don't make this more difficult for yourself.

- You're not crazy. Telling someone that your brain sometimes makes you feel like you're seeing things that aren't there, you're living in a dark well, or there are ants crawling up and down your spine doesn't mean your friend will brand you as a loon and ditch you for good. Remember, you're not crazy or weak or weird. Your symptoms in whatever way they manifest are happening to you, you didn't do anything to bring them on.

Friendship can scoop you out of a low mood, but friendship isn't about being each other's personal saviors. You can't magically fix someone's brain, and you can't always fix the shitty situation they're in. Friendship is about being there, about showing up, about listening, and about the little things. Just having a friend send me photos of cute dogs or a cucumber that looks remarkably like a large penis means a lot. Just having someone fill my in-box with things that make me laugh, no matter how childish, feels like they're there for me. They're not giving up.

> Friendship is about being there, about showing up, about listening.

My friends aren't trained therapists. I don't expect them to give me professional advice. Sometimes I'll explain how I'm feeling and they'll throw their hands up and say they genuinely have no idea what that feels like. I don't mind when they say that; it's not like they're shutting me down, they're just gently letting me know that I can't expect them to have a magic solution. A lot of this is new to them, and it's still quite new to me too.

Talking openly with your friends creates a dialogue that can often be surprising. When I told my best friend about my depression and how it was affecting my relationship at the time, it was like something clicked for her. She felt like she'd been going through the exact same thing and couldn't figure out what it was. She'd spent the last few weeks in bed wondering what the point of everything was. She'd requested a meeting with her tutor to drop out of her course, and she hadn't spoken to anyone in days. She hadn't reached out to anyone because she felt lost and ashamed. She'd chosen isolation to give herself space and time to figure out what was wrong, but got so used to her self-imposed solitude she couldn't get out of it. The escape route was blocked. She thought no one could help.

If I hadn't opened up about my own experience, she might not have had her aha moment. For her, knowing that she wasn't the only one who felt that way came as a giant relief. She wasn't dying, her body wasn't slowly decaying. She had depression and she needed to talk to someone about it.

We still discuss our brain blips when we're together. Sometimes I get so excited about the fact she's describing something that feels exactly like what I'm going through I give a little squeal. She gets me! What a wonderful woman! I sometimes send her a text that starts with: "Hey, do you ever feel . . . ?" or "Do you think it's normal that . . . ?" Having someone I can send a quick burst of a worry to is invaluable. She doesn't have to respond straightaway; just knowing that she'll read my query without judgment means everything.

Here are some things I wish people knew about my depression:

- I appreciate everything my friends and loved ones do for me and I'm sorry I'm not always able to show it.
- I appreciate you making the effort to come to my house, but don't show up unannounced because it makes me feel tense and ashamed of how I've neglected myself and my surroundings. I need a warning.
- If I seem distracted it's because half my head is filled with white noise.
- If possible, hang out with me one on one, because groups or new people freak me out
- I can watch a movie or TV show with you, but nothing too long or in depth, because my concentration probably isn't great
- Make plans with me—not big, life-changing ones, but little things like walks and picnics and going to the seaside. When I'm depressed, the future is a vast plane of nothingness; the more I can fill in the oppressive blanks, the more I'll be able to cling on to hope.
- When you say nice things to me I'm probably rolling my eyes or dismissing them, but I am genuinely grateful.
- Talking might be hard; sometimes it feels like there's a big blob of peanut butter in my mouth. So don't be scared if I don't say much or my words sound a bit garbled.

Friends are also able to give you a bit of perspective. My doomsday thinking often requires someone outside of my own head to give me an injection of realism. The way I tend to think and treat myself in my lowest mood is quite horrible, but I'm used to it; for me it's normal. I need a friend to make it clear to me that it's important I'm safe and well and I deserve better than self-destruction.

Go into the conversation with a good idea of what you want out of it. Is there something specific you could ask them to help with? No worries if there isn't; sometimes just sharing a situation with someone can make you feel lighter. If there is a more concrete thing your friend can help with, definitely mention that; they'll be eager to help out.

It could be something small, like asking them to call you so you get out of bed in time for an appointment. Or perhaps you just want them to sit and watch a movie with you once a week. Can they help you start a difficult conversation with your parents? Can they meet you after a therapy session so you have someone to talk to? If it's a big favor, keep in mind that they might say no. Don't see this as rejection. Maybe they had too much on their plate. Maybe they felt like they weren't the right person to help you.

As a caveat to all of this about how amazing friendship can be, there are times in our lives where it might feel that you simply don't have anyone close enough to you that you can talk to. That's OK. There's nothing wrong or broken about you.

If someone decides to tell you about their mental health issues and you're feeling a bit Oh-God-How-Will-I-Deal-With-This about it, here's some things to bear in mind:

- Your goal can't be to fix them. Even if you're unable to cheer them up, that isn't failing. Your goal is simply to listen.
- Just because you might see them smiling doesn't mean they're all of a sudden doing fine. Remember: people are excellent performers, and we select what we want to show the outside world.
- If someone doesn't respond to your messages or is a bit blunt when you ask if they're OK, don't jump to the conclusion that they're mad at you. Often it's because they

don't feel like they deserve your kind words so they block them out. Don't give up.

- If something is making you feel uncomfortable or you're worried, tell a third party; don't freak out and disappear.

- Remember that your friend is trying their best, even if it looks like they've put in minimal effort. They're really, really trying.

- Let them know you care, but don't pity them. Don't treat them like they're broken.

- Don't make them feel like their problems aren't valid: e.g., "A lot of people have it worse than you," or, "People are dying in Africa," or, "Well, maybe I should be the one cutting myself!" Your friend could be incredibly sensitive. While you're only human, try not to unleash any frustration. Don't snap and say things like: "Just get over it!" or "Just get out of bed for godsake"—this won't work. Tough love might work for personal trainers, but that's not a good foundation for friendship. A partner once said to me, "*You're* feeling suicidal? Your suicidalness is making *me* feel suicidal!" which did not go down well for us.

- Make them feel like you are a team and that you're in it together, even if they're the ones battling the demons.

- A simple spontaneous text can make someone's day.

- Remember it's OK to be scared. If your friend is severely depressed and their worldview is incredibly bleak, some of the things they might share with you can be shocking. You might even find yourself getting caught up in their way of thinking, and suddenly the world doesn't seem as bright as it did before. Make sure you have someone else you can talk to as well to offload when you need it.

▪ Get professional intervention. If your friend is talking about suicide and plans to kill themselves, it's not on you to stop them. You have to tell a relative or your local mental health facility, because their life could be in danger. You're not a trained psychologist, this isn't on you.

THERAPY

I've been in therapy on and off since I was sixteen. In total, I've seen seven different therapists, my favorite being the one I have at the time of writing this. She's very no-nonsense and doesn't let me get away with glossing over things that are really affecting me. I've had times where I've walked out of her offices thinking "She's a bitch, I hate her," and then I cool down and remember she's doing her job. She's able to rip the Band-Aid off even when it's clinging on for dear life.

My current therapy focuses on connecting current issues with larger themes in my life. There's a lot of introspection and talking about the past. I've had other types of therapy that were more practical, where we set goals and I had to carry out specific tasks between sessions. These tasks would be things like giving my mood a score, or pinpointing where in the day anxiety struck the most: what was I doing, what happened? These sessions used something called CBT, cognitive behavioral therapy, which is what GPs often recommend when you seek help for anxiety and depression.

Later on, I began seeing therapists who specialized in interpersonal therapy, where they go a little bit more into your childhood, relationship history, and your past in general. You get a lot of aha moments where suddenly a big chunk of what makes you you clicks into place. There are big things in your life that have significant impact on you that sometimes only someone with a bit of distance and a fresh perspective can point out (oh, and years of training).

There's lots of different types of therapy available, and before you settle on a therapist I recommend you do as much research as possible and try to figure out what will work for you. I ended up going from one to the other without putting much thought into why I chose a therapist. Often it was because I was using a free service—if you're finally at the top of a waiting list you don't want to be picky.

Don't do what I did. Instead of agreeing to whatever is made available to you, ask about the type of therapy being offered and Google it. CBT helped me set the foundation for getting my life back when anxiety was hell-bent on destroying it. It gave me tools and tricks to keep panic attacks under control—tools I still use to this day. Thanks to CBT methods, I was able to get out of my house, on a bus, and even to a party.

When I felt like I had the tools under my belt, I was eager to learn why my body reacts to certain situations in such a dramatic way. The more free-talking forms of therapy helped me do that. There's fewer take-home tips, but eventually I learned how to be more sympathetic to myself. My body isn't broken, my brain isn't sabotaging me; there are reasons I react the way I do.

Often the first session with your therapist will be a trial: you test out if the two of you get along and if it's likely the therapist will actually be able to help you. I never really paid too much attention to this part. It felt like I was having to regurgitate my life story, which I'd done many times before. If the therapist was nice and able to laugh at my dark humor, I thought we were pretty much compatible. I didn't pay attention to the details. Did I feel listened to? Did I feel comfortable? Were either of us more focused on the clock than on what was going on in the room?

While I have had some great therapists and counselors, not all of them have been right for me. My least favorite was a large man called Nigel with papery white skin that showed off every red blotch across his cheeks. I felt like he couldn't relate to my stories. I found myself changing my language, trying to avoid any judgment I suspected he was passing on me. It didn't help that instead of saying, "Are you promiscuous?" or "What is your attitude toward sex?" he'd say things like, "So how do you feel about sexy times?"

I've also had a therapist who I liked too much. I wanted to

be her friend outside of the tiny room we met in every Wednesday evening. When I was planning my solo trip to Paris I had to stop myself from inviting her along. She was warm and kind and gave me good advice. I transferred onto her the idea of what I thought a woman should be. She was put together, well adjusted, but also sympathetic and caring.

I wanted to please her so badly that whenever she'd make an observation about my life I'd eagerly nod and agree without actually thinking, "Wait, is this right?" I wanted so much to be a good client and I wanted her to feel like she was doing a good job. My instinct has always been to blend in with my surroundings, adapt, and be whatever the situation demands of me. It's how you survive, but this isn't ideal for therapy. My job isn't to protect the therapist's feelings or to make them feel good about their career choices.

So how do you know if you *have* found a good therapist?

Most important, you feel like you can share what you're feeling without fear of shame. This probably won't happen straightaway. In the beginning, I find myself talking about "easy" things: a stressful meeting I had, a difficult conversation, or a breakup that happened ages ago. These are easy for me because they're not at the top of my list of things that keep me awake at night. Once we get into a rhythm in our sessions, I peel my protective layers away and start divulging things that affect me more.

Shame is such a big part of my life. It engulfs me, pulls me away from healthy choices. It stuffs my throat with cotton wool and yaps at my ankles like a stray animal. When shame infiltrates therapy, it stops you from getting to the heart of what's troubling you. I found a way around when I started voicing the shame out loud, almost like breaking the fourth wall of therapy.

A session with my current therapist started as normal with a "How has your week been?" and to be frank, my week had been a disaster. I'd had too much to drink, fought with my boyfriend at the time—who I was pretty sure had a drug problem—and ended up in a hotel room in Shoreditch with an ex who I was having a toxic sexual text exchange with. I felt so ashamed about my actions and my lack of self-control. I didn't have a handle on anything, it seemed. I needed to vent, but I was scared my therapist would think I was a drunk, a whore, and, at best, morally bankrupt.

Instead of getting into what I wanted to say, I talked about a presentation I had to do at work. I felt like I hadn't performed well, but that it was OK because I'd also not smoked for three days, and I was getting stuck in a good book, so I had something to be proud of.

My therapist must have felt that between these two anecdotes was the weight of something else. She asked me to stop and explain what was going on in my head in that very moment. That to me felt easy. I just had to say what was going on in my mind.

"I feel a bit useless."

"Why is that?"

And here's where it got trickier.

"I want to tell you something that happened, but I'm worried you'll think I'm an awful person, even though I know it's your job to listen without judgment, and I'm not saying you're bad at your job, I'm just worried."

Then she said what has now become her catchphrase: "OK, there's a lot going on there."

We unpacked my sentence word by word and examined the feelings behind them. I realized that I was passing the shame I was feeling about myself on to her. Coming to this conclusion helped me untangle what I wanted to say from the webby strands of shame and I got it all out there.

Sometimes in therapy it can feel like it's a very routine exchange: your therapist asks you a question and you answer, but actually the hardest things to say don't come out that easily. Breaking the wall of therapy really helped me in that situation. It drove me away from that question-answer-question-answer structure. I was able to stop and share what I was feeling in the moment. Since then I've always paused the session when I felt the need to acknowledge when I feel awkward or fearful.

My therapist also asks me a lot about how I'm feeling physically, which helps me connect my mind and body. Often if I'm talking about something stressful I feel spaced out and floaty, so I need something to bring me back down to earth again.

Another thing I have learned not to do in therapy is treat it like a trial for a new stand-up routine. I consider myself to have a big Mary Poppins–style never-ending bag of flaws, but if I had to name one thing about myself I like it's that I know how to make people laugh. When friends are down I can comfort them and say something that'll make them smile, even just for a little bit. The problem for fans of humor though is that you use that humor in your storytelling all the time, even when it's perhaps not totally appropriate. In therapy, whenever I'm talking about self-harm or suicide or sexual assault, I inject a dark joke in there somewhere. It's more for my own protection than for anyone else's. I don't want it to get too serious, I don't want to think too much, and I don't want to feel sorry for myself. Ever.

This means that when a therapist laughed at one of my jokes or anecdotes I considered this to be a big win. I once made a counselor laugh three times in a row, and I walked out of there feeling like I'd just secured a spot on *SNL*. Turning my pain into laughter felt like a win. I was doing something productive. My therapist now (can you tell I'm mildly obsessed with her) has steered me away from using her as an audience member of *The Maggy Show*.

My therapist taught me to take my sessions more seriously. Before I start telling her something, I try to connect with how I really feel about it. It doesn't mean I then have to go ahead and talk in a sad, meek little voice. I still breeze through a lot of things, but I try to slow down. I find it hard to access my "real" feelings, the ones that are buried deep down somewhere, and I'm still not there, if I'm honest. But the more I slow down and try and notice what's going on, the closer I feel like I'm getting to achieving that.

THE WAITING GAME

In my quest to get my mental health back on track, I realized that there are *a lot* of phone calls involved. I hate speaking on the phone. I still have to take a deep breath before picking up, even if it's my boyfriend calling. So having to sort my life out by calling a dozen people, telling them all my problems and sometimes practically begging for help, isn't something I consider very fun.

So what do you do when you're between appointments and it feels like you have to wait a lifetime before you get any help?

■ Ask your doctor for a list of all the crisis numbers in your area you can call in an emergency situation where you're worried about what you might do to yourself. Put these in a folder and keep them somewhere safe. Some of them will be phone numbers you can call (e.g., your nearest emergency room), but others might be places you can walk in. My borough in London has what they call Crisis Cafe where you can go in to receive peer support in times of serious distress.

- Keep a diary of any appointments or phone assessments so you can follow up if they're going over the time within which they said they'd ring you back.
- Look for support groups in your area you can turn to if you feel comfortable in that kind of peer-to-peer setting.
- Keep a journal of thoughts, feelings, and moods to track how you're doing. That way, when you are finally at the top of a waiting list and you get seen, you can easily outline what's been going on for you in the recent months.
- Try out any mental health apps and websites you might find useful. I don't respond that well to apps, especially meditation ones, but while I was waiting for a therapist, I'd take an hour every Tuesday evening for an hour-long meditation session in the comfort of my living room. It gave me a sense of routine and structure. I felt like I was still doing something, despite being in limbo.
- Similarly, buy a book (buy my book—again!) and immerse yourself in writing that seems useful to you. Keep trying until you find something that sticks.
- Try to single out a block of time every day where all you do is relax, not working or online or stressing about anything. You're doing whatever it is that helps you zone out and breathe deeply: putting on face mask, wrapping yourself up in a duvet accompanied by a Harry Potter book, or chilling in the bath. Stick to this time. It's important.

MEDICATION

When I was first prescribed antidepressants, it happened very quickly. I spoke to my doctor about what was going on, she asked me a series of five questions, then prescribed me an SSRI.

I went home feeling extremely confused. This felt like a big deal. It felt like a massive life change I was embarking on, but it happened within the space of a few minutes. I collected my prescription from the pharmacy and put the pills down on my living room table. I talked it over with my college boyfriend, P., and we decided I should take them; they were a low dosage anyway, and if they weren't right for me I'd stop taking them. I swallowed my first pill and sat on our hand-me-down sofa waiting for something to happen.

A year later I went off them. My anxiety was nowhere near as bad, I was able to get on trains, I'd gotten a job and moved to London, and I was doing OK. Getting off them wasn't easy, however. My brain felt like street view on Google Maps when you click the arrow and the view moves in this slow, glitchy way. I'd be doing my job or getting ready for bed and a brain glitch occurred. It was scary, but it didn't last long; in a week or two I was back to leading my glitchless life.

About three years later, my anxiety had returned, together with deep depression and suicidal thoughts that hovered over me like a persistent cloud. I was given a new prescription,

this time a higher dosage. Because Citalopram had worked so well for me before, it seemed like a good choice.

A couple of months later, things hadn't really improved; my self-harm was out of hand and I kept getting flashing images of hurling my body in front of a car. My doctor upped my prescription. A couple of months later I came back and complained again about the self-harm, and they upped my dosage again.

I know from the outside this sounds like the doctors were just trying to silence me with pills, and to be honest it did feel like that. When you're desperate for a solution you'll take whatever your doctor will give you. But what I do know is that medication does genuinely help me. It makes me think more clearly so I have the headspace to counteract some of my intrusive thoughts. It also makes my anxiety symptoms more manageable.

Before you agree to take anything, look into what pills are being prescribed to you. This does unfortunately mean you have to navigate a gazillion scare stories about all the awful things that have happened to people on them. Do your research carefully, stick to outlets you trust, and don't let yourself get freaked out by other people's horror stories. Read medical sites and speak to helplines.

When your doctor is thinking about giving you medication, ask as many questions as possible so you don't go home and spend the whole night worrying. Ask what happens to your mood, your sex life, your physical health, and what will happen when you decide to stop taking them. Make sure you have follow-up appointments so you can check in with how you're doing.

Also, remember that there is no wonder pill that will cure your symptoms. When I received a diagnosis that was new to me—borderline personality disorder—I thought, "Well, at least I get to go on different meds now, and maybe this new one will make me happy instantly!" My psychiatrist told me that if I did want to change to stronger meds, I'd probably have trouble concentrating during the day. I shrugged and said I could deal with that, but asked what it would do for my reading. I was reading a book a day at that time; reading was everything.

"Oh, reading might be hard. Your brain might not be able to focus on all the words."

"Well screw that," I thought at that point. "I'll stick to what I'm doing. Reading is my natural antidepressant. I don't want to be without it."

There is also no one-size-fits-all pill. There are different types that work for different people, and sometimes it takes a bit of trial and error to find the one that is right for you. There's a period that usually lasts a few weeks where your body is adjusting and things get a bit wobblier at this time. Don't panic, this is normal.

> There is also no one-size-fits-all pill.

You also have to remember that you might not have to be on antidepressants your whole life. It's a bit like getting a cast when you break a leg. The cast is there to help you heal and to support your damaged leg. With the right lifestyle changes, physical therapy, and a good support network, the leg will heal and you can take that cast off.

Here are some things medication definitely isn't:

- It's not something you can only resort to when things get *really, really bad*. People who opt for meds aren't necessarily at breaking point, they just need some extra support.
- Meds aren't fake happiness. My meds don't give me a dose of fabricated emotions. I'm depressed, but I'm not a robot.

Meds pave a little way through the darkness to allow me to feel happiness, but they're not the happiness itself.

■ They don't change the fundamental things that make you who you are. They won't alter your personality. For me, meds help me realize who I am and who I could be if I work hard, get help, and am kind to myself.

■ Taking meds doesn't make you weak. It makes you proactive. You're taking charge of your situation.

■ Meds won't kill your creativity. Depression makes me unable to think imaginatively or even want to. Depression makes it so that I can't get out of bed or switch my laptop on to write something.

■ Your meds won't turn you into a raging drug addict.

■ Once you go off your meds you won't turn into a hysterical banshee. However, you might find that you'll end up crying a lot. Your brain may have been flattening out a lot of your emotions while you were medicated, so it needs a period of adjustment to figure out what kinds of responses are normal.

CHAPTER 13

Remember This When Things Are Getting Better

t had been a year since I burned my arm outside of the pub. Things were better, but I still felt the same. I felt like that sad, lost person. My wounds had healed, I didn't have to wear a sleeve of bandages anymore, but I felt listless and tired of being tired.

A group of friends were having a birthday party that I wanted to go to. My dating life was in a bit of a shambles and I wanted to be around people who could make me laugh (and potentially post a pic of me laughing so the guy I was dating would see all the great fun I was having without him). The group of friends decided they wanted to go to the exact same pub I'd been to that fateful evening a year before. Apparently there aren't enough pubs in Stoke Newington that London media people like to go to.

An itching optimism within me made me feel like it would be all right to go. At the very least, it was a better option than staying home pining over some guy I didn't think liked me. No one there would know what had happened the last time I'd been to that pub, but for safety I went with my friend who *had* been there. He knew this place would be a bit of a minefield for me, so he became my fire exit. If I needed a quick escape I could use him.

Getting ready for this party felt like preparing for battle. There were things I needed to have in place. I told myself I couldn't smoke or drink too much (after two glasses of wine I was going to switch to Diet Coke). I also felt like I needed to arm myself with things that *were* going to be productive. I stuck on a YouTube tutorial and caked myself in makeup. Foundation and concealer were my camouflage. They made me feel powerful, like I was ready for anything. I wore a dress I loved and some fancy shoes, and I went to my friend's beforehand so we could go in together. I had a water bottle and some gum in my bag, and a book in case I needed to go off and read. You never know.

I felt a shiver when I walked in, past the flicker of fairy lights. The pub was full of people and the odd dog here and there. My friends had a swarm of other friends around them, so if I needed to bail I could go relatively unnoticed. There was nothing tying me to the pub, I wasn't trapped. I was in there by my own volition. I could leave when I wanted to: I was in control.

I took a seat on the fringes of the group and tried to settle into the conversation. Most of these friends were from work, so it was easy to go into office politics and the new office fridge and how terrible the sofa in reception was. While everyone chipped in, I glanced behind me. There was the table I'd been sitting at a year ago. Tonight it was occupied by a couple sharing a bottle of red wine. They looked so calm, like they'd decided to go for a drink before returning home to a night of watching episodes of a show they loved. Their peacefulness seemed so unlike anything I had felt when I had been sitting there myself.

Someone asked me what I'd been doing with my weekend so far and I reeled myself back into the conversation. I said something about watching a true crime documentary and returned the question. It was a bit like playing that hot potato game in school, when you stand in a circle and everyone tosses a little beanbag around until the music stops. Whoever has the "hot potato" in their hand has to leave the game. For me, having to lead the conversation was that hot potato. This night was stressful enough; I just wanted to lean back and listen to everyone else talk. I also needed enough space to tackle those intrusive thoughts should they arise.

Sitting, listening, and sipping my wine slowly helped me last two hours without any freak-outs. My only issue was that I was tired, and I could feel my eyelids drooping a little. The friend who'd come to the party with me suggested we go back home and I felt like I was ready. We watched the true crime documentary. We toasted with a big bag of hummus chips and cans of Coke. I'd made it. I proved to myself I could handle a stressful situation. I rode it out. I was kind to myself and I caught up with my friends. I did it.

For me, the notion of "recovery" is having several experiences like the one I just described. But it's not always going to be foolproof. Recovery isn't a before-and-after photo. It's not a straightforward journey from one point to another. There are times I get pulled back in, when I seem to shake off everything I've learned. There are times even now I return to self-harming, I drink too much, I act irrationally or dangerously, I push someone away. Usually in the aftermath of these times I make it worse by scolding myself for not having learned anything. I hurt myself and look in the mirror and think: "Come on, surely I'm too old for this shit. Don't I know better?"

> Recovery isn't a before-and-after photo.

Just because I have all the tools doesn't mean I'll always know exactly how to use them. However, with each setback, the time it takes for me to regain control, to find the right tool, decreases. Instead of full months spiraling out of control,

I can limit it to weeks. Sometimes I can recognize the symptoms and get ready. Prepare for battle.

I'm also coming to understand that my brain isn't my enemy. There are times when anxiety, for example, has actively protected me. When my uncle passed away after a brave and devastating battle with cancer, I returned to the Netherlands for his funeral. With my dad and siblings beside me, we were part of the procession walking into the church. It was incredibly hard seeing the pain among my uncle's immediate family— my cousins and aunty and my dad, his brother.

I turned away from my dad, who was blinking away tears. I looked around me and noticed how many people were there. There must have been hundreds. My brain decided to tell me it would be really, really awful if I tripped right now. Can you imagine? What if I tripped someone else too, and they tripped someone, and *boom*, the coffin would fall. It would all be my fault!

When I made it to my seat unscathed I still couldn't relax. All the usual fears came up: imagine if you vomit right now, imagine if you pass out, everyone will think you're such a drama queen, everyone will think you're trying to steal the limelight at a fucking funeral.

I knew I couldn't give in to my fears. I had to be there. I couldn't run off. My siblings were on one side of me and my dad on the other. I tried to remember what I'd learned. I got out my mental toolkit. OK, breathe. Breathe properly. I filled my lungs with air and let it out, slowly, through my mouth. I relaxed my shoulders, clenched and unclenched my fists, and told myself to ride it out. And I did.

After the funeral it took a few days for me to shake the nervous tension I'd carried since the church. When I flew back to London it slowly melted like snow at the end of winter. Day by day it disappeared a little until it seemed to be gone completely. It was then that it suddenly hit me. The fog cleared and there was one resounding message for my brain to tackle: my uncle is dead. My dad didn't have a brother anymore. My aunty had lost her husband and my cousins their dad. Not to mention the hundreds of people in the church, they'd all lost someone too.

I can't grieve around other people. I sneak off to quiet corners and cry by myself. That day at the church, my anxiety had given me something to focus on, to put all my attention on until I was ready to let go and to feel the weight of my uncle's passing. I was weirdly grateful for my strange brain. For once it was trying to do me a favor.

RECOVERY

Recovery is about learning, about moving forward one step at a time. When I have a setback, I find myself completely absorbed in negativity; it rolls around my head like laundry in the washing machine. Everything is shrouded in a dark haze.

I find it hard to feel just a little bit bad. It's always a near-catastrophic *end-of-the-world* feeling for me.

As I'm trying to get better, I've found it incredibly important to cling on to the little things that make me happy. Small steps I can make to offer myself a rope and dig my mind out of its black hole. Here are some of those things I've found I can lean on to make the catastrophe feel a little less catastrophic:

Lists

You've made it this far in the book, so you've probably gathered I appreciate a good list. I can't say enough good things about them. Lists impose a sense of organization; without lists I feel totally adrift.

My room is a burial site for completed and half-completed lists. There's not a day that goes by without some kind of list making. Even on vacation I make a list of the books I want to read, or how long I want to suntan for before I get a heat rash. Lists break down the stickier problems in life: "Make more money" becomes slightly more attainable when you read it as "pitch freelance articles to so-and-so"; "make all your lunches for the week on a Sunday"; "chase old housemate for the money they owe."

I can divide my lists into the future and the past. Goals

and to-do lists are about the future, even if it's as immediate as what I'm going to be doing in the next half hour. Some lists act as a little stepladder into the past. I'll make a list of all the things I think have been bothering me that day. What am I hung up on? What's making me feel uncomfortable? What does this feeling remind me of?

It's funny that my first big job at BuzzFeed involved making lists. As a staff writer I'd take some kind of identity fixture—"being shy" or "being a bookworm" or "being the eldest sibling"— and break those things down into a variety of headings. Plenty of people look down on this style of writing, but doing this for almost three years taught me that lists tell a story. OK, not a big exploration into the human psyche type story, but the BuzzFeed-style list has a narrative, a start and a finish.

This is how I approach lists outside of BuzzFeed too. I imagine myself at the end, once I've completed the tasks and deadlines. How will I feel at the end? How can I achieve that feeling?

When I used to own *The Sims* (I'm yet to find a laptop fast enough to continue playing my beloved game), I had a very particular way of playing. I'd take a character (usually remarkably similar to myself or someone I wanted to sleep with). Press pause. Fill up the top screen with actions I wanted them to undertake. Then I'd hit play and just sit there and watch the actions unfold—hopefully getting that red bar back to green, or finally getting that couple to make a baby. It stressed me out clicking the actions while the game was in play mode. I needed that time to pause, to think. I also wanted to revel in that almost euphoric relief I felt just after I'd planned a set of actions. I've done the hard bit now, the worst is over. Let's see the results.

I am my own Sim. Sometimes this approach feels a bit robotic, but it gives me that sense of control. Even on a day where I have absolutely nothing to do, a lazy Sunday morning, where my only task is relieving my bladder whenever I can be bothered to get out of bed, even on days like that I'll make a list. It might say: "Finish reading that chapter, read that gossip blog, send your friend a dog meme." None of that is particularly hard to achieve, but it makes me feel good that I have.

Lists also help me create a sense of continuity. For me, depression and dissociation blur the day into a cloud of nothingness. I've had days where I've had to stop what I'm doing just to lie down on the floor. It's not that I'm tired, it's just that there seems to be no possible way to continue with what I'm doing. Instead I just lie there completely still. The only way to climb out of this state is to get thinking about a list of things to do. Just keep going. Do that one thing. Go from the beginning to the end. You can do it.

Phone Apps

My phone casts a lot of "bad vibes." I can be in a perfectly good mood and decide to look at what that girl who may or may not be dating my ex is up to, and suddenly my soul feels obliterated. After the breakup with Casanova guy from the theater, I was left reeling more than usual and I found myself unable to stop thinking about him. It colonized every inch of my brain. I replayed the breakup over and over again. I went over everything I'd done to make him break up with me. I went over everything I said. He wanted space from me and we weren't speaking, so my thoughts had nowhere to go but swarm around my skull.

I tried to get out of the house. I went to a play with an old friend and tried to see an exhibition by my favorite photographer, but nothing helped. Everything reminded me of him— every place, every image—until eventually I gave up, went home, and completely gave in to the breakup loop.

On the train home from an exhibition by William Burroughs (who was always my problematic literary crush), I felt defeated by another utterly useless afternoon of not being able to connect to something I was so passionate about. I watched the guy next to me play Candy Crush. I hadn't thought about that game in a while. I'd obsessively played for a month and given up, thanks to all the extra features they make you pay for.

On the spot I downloaded it from my app store and started playing. The initial levels are quite easy to pass, so I got an instant dose of satisfaction. From then on it's mostly luck. Correct me if you're a Candy Crush pro, but there's not a tremendous amount of skill involved.

Before I knew it, my train had reached its station and I

hadn't thought about my ex at all. It was nighttime and I realized I hadn't cried since the exhibition. This was progress! A friend texted asking if I was OK and I replied, "Hanging in there X," which was the most positive response I'd had for anyone in weeks. I went back to my game and played until 3 a.m., and then I slept. I dreamed of bulging candies bursting happily over my head.

I eventually kicked the Crush habit once my brain stopped obsessing about my ex on its own accord. I started reading again, watching movies properly, and even writing slightly angsty poems—but it helped.

I'm definitely not suggesting you will your depression away by spending every second of the day on a game on your phone. For me, deleting the usual social media suspects that make me feel like shit and instead spending my time bursting candy canes was a definite improvement. It gave me some structure to the day, and I was able to get out of bed and on the train. It even gave me something to look forward to. I ended up getting to level 90. I don't know if that's good, please don't tell me if it's not.

Dogs

When I see a dog, a part of my brain emits a high-pitched squeal, and all I can think about is getting as close to that dog as possible. Best-case scenario is that I get to pet the dog, but if there are things in the way or the owner seems particularly wearied by a deranged blond lady running up to their pet, I can be content with just seeing the dog.

No dog is like another; they're so unique, contradictory, and clever. I like old dogs the most. Dogs that have lived a little, that give you the impression they can tell you stories from the Great Dog War of '09. I love dogs who want to protect you a little, who know when you're sad and rest their head on your lap.

One of the nicest things anyone has ever done for me involves a dog. It was after my sexual assault, recurring visits to the ER, and a bout of depression that brought me so low I didn't know how I was going to claw myself out again.

My friend D. told me to come meet him in Crouch End, which was pretty far away from where I lived. I didn't want to leave the house, let alone make a long journey through London. My brain was overly sensitive to stimuli. Just the idea of crossing the road made my head hurt. However, D. insisted, and I knew deep down I needed to be around people. I'd been left alone to my own devices for too long and it wasn't looking pretty.

I got up and put on a bleach-stained hoodie that used to belong to my mum. I hoped I didn't bump into anyone on my way there. When I got to Finsbury Park I met D., and we took a bus farther north to Crouch End. While he talked, I put my head on his shoulder and pretended I was still in bed.

At Crouch End we sat and chatted on a park bench for a bit. I was getting increasingly annoyed—I could've sat on a park bench nearer to my house. When it hit 2 p.m., D. got a text and I made some joke that if he was going to text one of his many female admirers I was going to go home.

He ignored me and made me follow him across the street toward a house on the corner. I still had no idea what was going on. I was pretty sure he didn't know anyone in Crouch End, especially not someone who owned this beautiful mansion. An incredibly glamorous lady opened the door. She had golden hair that resembled the color of my own, when I actually washed it. She said hi to D., and then handed us the most beautiful golden retriever I'd ever seen in my life. "Thanks for walking Milo," she said. "Bring him back whenever you're done, no rush!"

She closed the door and I stared at D., not quite believing that my favorite ever animal in the whole world was currently sniffing my battered Converse shoes: "Is this real?"

"Yep, let's go walk Milo."

Turns out D., a keen user of dating apps, had finally found an app that is worth everyone's time: Borrow My Doggy. It's an app where dog owners and dog lovers can connect and help each other out. D. had walked Milo before, and his owners were so pleased they let D. come over and take Milo whenever he wanted.

Milo was a wonderful creature. I made D. hold him on

the leash so I could spend my time running ahead and staring at his wonderful face. When we walked around the park I was astounded that some people walked past without even noticing him. I felt like shouting, "Come on, people! Look at this beautiful dog. Look at him!"

At the park café, Milo sat patiently by us while we ate sandwiches. For me, the magic of Milo was that he demanded all of my attention—not because he was a hassle, but because he was so beautiful and gentle, and I couldn't stop staring at him. My whole focus was on seeing what he was doing, what his expression was, how he was walking, what he was smelling. He was a little escape path out of my depression, even if it was just for a day.

The rest of the afternoon was pure joy. It made me think about the future—perhaps I'd own a dog like Milo one day. Walking Milo helped me get out and stretch my legs and breathe in some air that hadn't been trapped in my room for weeks.

If someone you love is struggling (and they happen to be animal lovers) take them to the zoo or the aquarium on a quiet day in the week. Go walk a dog or visit a farm. Remind them that animals exist, and loving animals is such a simple yet restorative thing. Milo reminded me of all the dogs of my childhood—the ones who saw me cry, who caught my tennis balls. Milo also gave me a well-needed break from myself for a bit. Hope you're reading this, Milo.

Law & Order

A lot of TV shows are available for binge watching, giving you the option to watch the entire thing from start to finish in one go without eating properly or getting dressed. You can just sit there, becoming one with your couch, only occasionally reminding yourself you need to pee.

There's a comfort for me in bingeing when I'm depressed that I don't think is all bad. When my head is filled with static, it's impossible to concentrate on anything. I *can't* read, I can't sleep, and I can't listen to anyone. What I can do is follow a TV show that I've either seen many times before— something like *Seinfeld* or *Parks and Recreation*—or a TV show that's very formulaic; something that involves solving a case or a crime like *Law & Order* or *The Good Wife*.

For me, watching a show like *Parks and Rec* feels like coming home. I enter the world of Pawnee like I'm back at my family home for the holidays. I know the place well, I know the characters and their stories. I know which jokes make me cry from laughing, and I know which episodes to skip because the plotline isn't as great as the others. There's also not a risk that I'll overdose. There won't be any new *Parks and Rec*s, there's no direct impulse to get to the end. When I do, I can just start all over again, no big deal.

With the second type of shows, the *Law & Order*s of the world, I'm comforted by the fact that *most* cases are solved and things tend to be wrapped up quite neatly. The show isn't exactly lighthearted viewing; it gets a lot of its inspiration from real-life tragedies happening in crime-riddled cities across America, but *Law & Order* has a narrative structure you can rely on. It's easily digestible.

The other thing I like about shows like *Law & Order*, *Criminal Minds*, *Firefly*, or even *The Simpsons* is that they're episodic, which means they're self-contained. Every time you nestle in to watch an episode, you're welcomed with conflict and resolution. You can also jump in at any point and jump around seasons, and you can fall back into it wherever you want. There are also a *lot* of episodes of *Law & Order*, which makes me feel calm. I don't have the pressure of *having* to finish an entire season in one weekend because there's still loads to go. My brain likes the shows; it likes skipping from one problem to the next without having to solve it myself. There's amazing detectives to do that stuff.

From trying to keep track of all the things that make me feel good—dogs, TV shows, games—I've realized how much all of the little things make me feel alive and how much I want to stay alive, despite everything. Even in my darkest moments—on the side of the Tube platform or with a razor blade to my wrist—I have a well inside me that's all about life. I want to taste, and feel, and touch things. I want to be remembered. I want to help other people, and I really want to be able to help myself. There's no way I can look at all the effort I've put into getting better and think, "Wow, what a slacker." I've done a lot, and I will keep doing a lot, and I'm proud of how committed and dedicated I am to my own aliveness.

I know that underneath all my issues there's a person who loves living. She likes zip wires and sharks and wild swimming and the first time a baby laughs. I try to activate that part as much as I can, even though it's especially hard when depression hits me like a ton of bricks and the alive part of me lies dormant until the storm passes. Feeling alive largely means enjoying something new. Something that involves challenging my brain or challenging my body. Newness makes me feel refreshed, learning a new skill makes me feel proud. Even when I try something and immediately fail at it (e.g., the time I took an acrobatics class), I go home remembering how much fun I had.

Some other things that make me feel more alive:

- Licorice that's so salty you have to suck on your tongue afterward
- Having a warm shower and walking around the house buck naked afterward
- Painting my toenails a neon color
- Reading a poem that's so good it crashes straight into my skull
- Writing my own poem that's definitely not as good, but it doesn't matter
- Lying flat on the floor listening to Radiohead in the dark
- Jumping into an ice-cold pond
- Lasting longer than I usually do in that ice-cold pond
- Doing a shoulder stand
- Doing a shoulder stand and not toppling over
- Going for a walk first thing in the morning
- Taking a train to a new city, getting out of the station, and having no idea what to expect from my surroundings
- Photographing my friends in the woods when the sun is setting
- Swimming with friends where the exercise is actually coming from all the laughter rather than from the swimming
- Cycling slowly in the rain

- Cycling fast through empty streets at midnight
- Cycling fast and singing "Creep" at the top of my lungs
- Having an incredible orgasm and lying there afterward until it slowly subsides and everything feels easy
- Going to a concert and daring myself to inch closer to the front with every song
- Running into the sea in one go rather than dipping my toes in one by one
- Cooking a three-course meal for someone
- Seeing a work of art that makes me stand and stare until my back hurts
- That initial rushing feeling of walking into a roaringly packed football stadium
- Joining a march or a protest
- Making up a song from scratch, preferably in the shower
- Disembarking a roller coaster and not quite believing I just survived that triple corkscrew
- Spotting family waiting for me at the arrivals gate of an airport
- Going to see a play that makes me cry
- Hugging a dog I haven't met before
- Hugging a dog I have met before
- Hugging a dog, any dog, every dog

CHAPTER 14

Remember This
When You're Sad

Big girls don't cry—they fucking howl, wail, sob, yowl, pour buckets of tears out into the streets until there's a flood.

I cry all the time, and not just because of my mental health issues. In fact, my depression rarely makes me cry. Depression yanks the visceral emotions out of me and replaces them with a cold mist that haunts the corridors of my body. I cry because I'm sensitive, because things get to me easily, and because sometimes I enjoy sitting in the bathtub in just a puddle of water and crying my fucking heart out. Some people love walking around naked or furiously masturbating. I love having a cry.

Thanks to Facebook I cry daily. People love sharing emotional videos about people overcoming incredible feats. I've spent a lot of my career making some of those videos—I know exactly how they work, what's going to get to people—and yet I'm not immune. There's a type of emotional videos that always get to me. It's not old people; I don't cry when I see cute grandpas (sorry). They're ones where dads do nice things for their kids.

I know it shouldn't be that magical, a dad doing a nice thing for their child, mums do nice things for their kids all the time, and they don't have twenty-something women crying about it at their desk. Whatever, I'm only human. There's a video where a dad gives his toddler daughter a motivational speech in the mirror, and soon enough my keyboard was drenched in all the saltwater that leaked out of my eyes.

I cry offline too. Just as easily. I once cried because I kicked a pebble onto the road and a car ran over it and I told myself I was a mass-murdering pebblist. I also cry when things don't go my way: when I leave my bankcard at home; when I go to my friend's house to stay the night and forget to pack my meds; or when someone shoves me on the escalator.

Sometimes my reasons for crying aren't especially good ones (the pebble for example), but the second I feel my eyes well up there's absolutely nothing I can do to stop the tear train. In the summer I enjoy the perk of wearing XXL shades to hide my outpourings of sadness. In the winter it's trickier, but I can often blame it on a sharp wind.

I'm so dedicated to the crying because I started jotting down all the places in public that let me have a good, satisfying weep. These places were useful for being either discreet, comfortable, or a perfect match for my miserable mood. See if any of them work for you:

- At the front of the bus on the top level
- In a Bikram yoga class
- In the back of an Uber
- In the self-help section of your favorite bookshop
- Alone in a rowboat in a romantic park
- In a modern art museum
- In the queue for the post office
- In the queue for airport security
- In the queue for the night bus
- In an empty cinema
- In a McDonald's ball pit
- In your shower
- In your gym's shower
- In any goddamn shower
- By a self-checkout machine
- On top of a clock tower
- By the big copy machine at your work
- By the ready-made meals in your local supermarket

- On a roller coaster
- On a water slide
- At a dog show
- In a garden center where you can blame your allergies
- In the bridal section of a department store
- On a pier
- During a massage
- In the back of a bar under a table
- In the hairdresser's after they show you what your new hair looks like
- In Ikea; anywhere will do, but bonus points if you can make it to the warehouse section at the end where everyone is so exhausted you won't be the only one crying

The reason I'm babbling about crying is that I don't see anything wrong with it. I'm an emotional wreck most days. I can go from feeling like I'm owning everything to, in the next minute, despairing that my life is shit and nothing good will ever happen. It's very likely I'm going to be able to manage my emotions even better than I do now, but it's less likely I'm going to change fully. I'm always going to be what some have said is "a bit much," "a bit intense." People have called me crazy, unstable, destructive, a burden, and irresponsible. The gem: "You are going to die alone."

Well, maybe I might, but I'm going to make the absolute best of it until I do. I'm going to be as alive as I possibly can be. I'm going to take risks and take care of myself and the people I love, and when it feels safe, every so often I'm going to let go and fall back into the world and see what the world has to offer for me.

> I'm going to be as alive as I possibly can be.

When I was fourteen years old, before a lot of the disordered eating and self-harm started, I'd just come back from prom at a school I'd just started. We were living in Doha in Qatar in a compound filled with Range Rovers and maids and private pools. It was a strange world, and it wouldn't be my world for long. A friend had dropped me off, and before I decided to go into my house to say hi to my parents, I went to the compound's public pool.

I was still wearing my prom dress; it was orange with a black band around the waist. I felt pretty, maybe even a bit glamorous. I liked the dress on me. I'd been flirting with a blond-haired boy called Max I fancied. I'd been one of the first people to dance, and I just felt really exhilarated about the whole evening. No one was at the pool, it was late, and the darkness cloaked the place like a dome.

I walked to the edge of the pool and turned around. My brain was clinging to the last song I'd danced to: "Baby If You Give It to Me," by Busta Rhymes and Mariah Carey. I

hummed the song to myself until I let the lyrics go, like I was blowing a dandelion into the wind. I closed my eyes, took a deep breath, and let myself fall backward into the lukewarm water. I floated around on my back looking at the sky like it was the roof of my house. When I grew tired, I climbed out and took my dress off and wrapped myself in a rogue towel that had been left behind by someone and walked back to my house smiling at my little adventure.

For me, that feeling by the swimming pool is something I remember when things are rough: a feeling of exuberant abandonment, letting go, and being just that little bit proud of myself. Some people wish to return to the safety of the womb. I want to return to the safety of that night. When I was young and ridiculous and filled with optimism.

When I'm sad—not weepy, but properly fucking miserable— I remember how lucky I am I still have so many pools to fall backward into. I have new journeys to make and stories to tell. I can't rewrite my past, but I can use it as a guide for my future. I have an infinite amount of books to read and music to discover. I can get lost in the beauty of small things: a line in someone's brow, a dimple, a postcard, an orange peel, a jar of pencil shavings. There is so much I haven't encountered yet. There are so many breaths that are waiting to be taken away. I have loved and I'm able to love and I'll keep learning how to love even better than I do now.

The future is exciting, but the present can be just as thrilling if only I let it. Life is full of change and so am I. I can alter my perspective, my behavior. I can regenerate. I can improve. I can work hard. I am brave, sometimes I am strong, and I'm grateful for both of those qualities. I've been through things I never thought I'd overcome.

So remember this: life is fucking hard sometimes, but if you just keep going, just like you kept turning the pages in this book, you'll be OK.

Acknowledgments

A couple years ago Laura Williams approached me about becoming my agent and my first reaction was "WHYHHHYYYYYYY!?!" until I stopped nervous screaming and said yes. This pretty much sums our relationship. Laura tells me about a great opportunity, I stare at her in terror and she convinces me that I should go for it and it's a good thing. Thanks to Laura's support as an agent and friend I was able to complete this book without dying from anxiety in the process. Also thanks to everyone else at PFD, especially Marilia, who has been nothing but supportive and enthusiastic and is an absolute babe.

Acknowledgments

Thank you to everyone at Bonnier: Natalie, Ellis, September, and the eagle-eyed copy editors. Thank you to Morwenna, who sent me a lovely email after reading my first draft when I was feeling very "ugh this book is dumb." It really put the spark back into my brain. Thank you.

Sladjana over at Unieboek | Het Spectrum, aka the boss queen of the Dutch publishing industry—thank you!!! Sladjana has been a champion of my ideas and my very existence since the day we met. Thank you for making me feel like a rock star every time I'm with you.

Special thanks to all the comrades I met at BuzzFeed. When my brain decided to do a nosedive into hell there were some fantastic people who dug me out of despair. I can't thank you enough. I love you Kim, Kelly, Francis, Laura G, Rcmcc (for realizing things), Gena (for speaking things into existence), Hannah (for paving the way with your iconic book and badassery). Big love to Victoria for trusting me and being a fellow anxious bee. Thank you to everyone in the union chat group. Thank you to all of you who sent kind messages and had my back. I will never, ever forget. Thank you Paul Hamilos for taking me out to that Korean place and telling me in the kindest way possible to get my shit together. Thank you for telling me about your own mental health. Thank you for making me feel less alone. Thank you Dan. Sorry you had to be there in my ugliest hour. Thank you for literally picking me up. Thank you for not letting go.

Thanks to everyone I've ever spoken to online about mental health: on Instagram, Twitter, Facebook groups, Reddit, and in the comments of some of my BuzzFeed posts. Thank you for making me feel like I was doing something important. Thank you to my therapist Susannah who has given me a handle on my life. Thanks for teaching me how to be less of a dick to myself.

Thank you to new friends I've made at the BBC. Thanks Megha for letting me vent and thanks for never judging. Thanks to the very cool team at BBC Studios Digital. Thanks for being supportive about my book. Thanks for letting me work on the 1 in 4 campaign. It meant so much to be part of it.

Thanks to wonderful Flo who elevated this book with her illustrations. Thank you for being so excited about this project from the start. Thanks for going on this trip with me. Thanks for laughing at all my jokes even when they're fucking weird. Thanks for making me feel good about myself. You're one of a kind. I love you dearly.

Thank you to my amazing friend Laura Brouwer who is so talented and beautiful and intelligent and beautiful and kind and beautiful (yes I'm totally in love with you). Thank you for always being proud of me. You are my family. Thank you Vi, the crazy French lady. You always know what to say and you always always have my back. Thank you Ilavda who taught me so many things it's ridiculous. Thanks for always being there when I need help with my vagina and my brain. Thanks for introducing me to the BPD Reddit thread when I was desperate for people who'd understand. Thanks for being unashamedly honest and brave. You're a fucking icon.

Thank you to my fantastic family. Mum, Dad, Rein, Sandy, Annie, and Tim. I know it's not easy reading a lot of this stuff and thank you for sticking by me and lifting me up. Sandy you're a dreamboat of a little brother. I love you. You're so bloody wise— how are you only twelve years old (kidding!). Annie you will always be my favorite role model. You are the most incredible woman. I'm lucky to be related to you. Thank you to Alex's parents: Chris and Pat. Thank you for saying such lovely things about my writing.

Thank you Jay, aka Amaroun, you're so unbelievably talented and kind to me! Thanks to Cord and Rik who let me do a lot of writing in their house and use their hot water. Thank you Rik for giving me the idea of a book launch and I guess you can come if you want, whatever, ugh.

To my boyfriend, Alex: thanks for everything. OK, bye!!

LOL. Alex. God damnit. There's too much to say. You're so handsome it's too much. Thanks for being a sounding board for every thought that enters my head. Thanks for being totally chill and supportive when I asked you to read my first draft. Let's face it a lot of this book talks about other dudes I boned, which isn't fun to read. Thanks for being so filled with kindness and love and being so generous with that love. Thanks for being patient, especially with my BPD, which is kind of like dating a woman with a poisonous sea urchin for a heart. I know the main way I show you I love you is by wrestling you to the ground or prodding your belly button or shouting inappropriate things in public places but jokes aside: I'm completely overwhelmed by how much you changed my life for the better. You made me realize I can be more than someone's "crazy ex-girlfriend"—I can be someone's crazy current girlfriend and sometimes I can even be just a girlfriend full stop.

And last, to everyone who has found themselves in the pages of this book. You're not broken. You're not losing it. Keep going. Take baby steps. Be kind to yourself and don't forget to go out there and pet as many dogs as you can.

ABOUT THE AUTHOR

Originally from the Netherlands, Maggy moved to London to complete her MA in writing for stage and broadcast media at the Royal Central School of Speech and Drama. She spent a few years freelancing and selling Häagen-Dazs in West End theaters until she became the Social Media Editor for Buzz-Feed. She now works as a Social Manager for BBC Three.

Maggy has been writing about mental health for five years, and helped the BBC launch their 1 in 4 campaign during their mental health season. Maggy is based in London, and you can connect with her on Twitter @Maggyvaneijk.